WISHES
FULFILLED

OTHER HAY HOUSE PRODUCTS BY DR. WAYNE W. DYER

BOOKS

Being in Balance
Change Your Thoughts—Change Your Life
Don't Die with Your Music Still in You (with Serena J. Dyer) (available June 2013)
Everyday Wisdom
Everyday Wisdom for Success
Getting in the Gap (book-with-CD)
I Am (children's book with Kristina Tracy)
Incredible You! (children's book with Kristina Tracy)
Inspiration
The Invisible Force
It's Not What You've Got! (children's book with Kristina Tracy)
Living the Wisdom of the Tao
My Greatest Teacher (with Lynn Lauber)
No Excuses! (children's book with Kristina Tracy)
The Power of Intention
The Power of Intention gift edition
A Promise Is a Promise
The Shift
Staying on the Path
10 Secrets for Success and Inner Peace
Stop the Excuses!
Unstoppable Me! (children's book with Kristina Tracy)
Your Ultimate Calling

AUDIO/CD PROGRAMS

Advancing Your Spirit (with Marianne Williamson)
Applying the 10 Secrets for Success and Inner Peace
The Caroline Myss & Wayne Dyer Seminar
Change Your Thoughts—Change Your Life (unabridged audio book)
Change Your Thoughts Meditation
Everyday Wisdom (audio book)
Excuses Begone! (available as an audio book and a lecture)
How to Get What You Really, Really, Really, Really Want
I AM Wishes Fulfilled Meditation (with James Twyman)
Inspiration (abridged 4-CD set)
Inspirational Thoughts
Making the Shift (6-CD set)

Making Your Thoughts Work for You (with Byron Katie)
Meditations for Manifesting
101 Ways to Transform Your Life (audio book)
The Power of Intention (abridged 4-CD set)
A Promise Is a Promise (audio book)
Secrets of Manifesting
The Secrets of the Power of Intention (6-CD set)
10 Secrets for Success and Inner Peace
There Is a Spiritual Solution to Every Problem
The Wayne Dyer Audio Collection/CD Collection
Wishes Fulfilled (unabridged audio book)
Your Journey to Enlightenment (6-tape program)

DVDs

Change Your Thoughts—Change Your Life
Excuses Begone!
Experiencing the Miraculous
Inspiration
My Greatest Teacher (a film with bonus material featuring Wayne)
The Power of Intention
The Shift, the movie (available as a 1-DVD program and an expanded 2-DVD set)
10 Secrets for Success and Inner Peace
There's a Spiritual Solution to Every Problem
Wishes Fulfilled

MISCELLANEOUS

Change Your Thoughts—Change Your Life Perpetual Flip Calendar
Everyday Wisdom Perpetual Flip Calendar
Inner Peace Cards
Inspiration Perpetual Flip Calendar
The Power of Intention Cards
The Power of Intention Perpetual Flip Calendar
The Shift Box Set (includes *The Shift* DVD and *The Shift* tradepaper book)
10 Secrets for Success and Inner Peace Cards
10 Secrets for Success and Inner Peace gift products: *Notecards, Candle,* and *Journal*

All of the above are available at your
local bookstore, or may be ordered by visiting:

Hay House UK: **www.hayhouse.co.uk**
Hay House USA: **www.hayhouse.com**®
Hay House Australia: **www.hayhouse.com.au**
Hay House South Africa: **www.hayhouse.co.za**
Hay House India: **www.hayhouse.co.in**

WISHES FULFILLED

MASTERING THE ART OF
MANIFESTING

Dr Wayne W. Dyer

HAY HOUSE

Australia • Canada • Hong Kong • India
South Africa • United Kingdom • United States

First published and distributed in the United Kingdom by:
Hay House UK Ltd, Astley House, 33 Notting Hill Gate, London W11 3JQ.
Tel.: (44) 20 3675 2450; Fax: (44) 20 3675 2451;. www.hayhouse.co.uk

Published and distributed in the United States of America by:
Hay House, Inc., PO Box 5100, Carlsbad, CA 92018-5100. Tel.: (1) 760 431 7695 or
(800) 654 5126; Fax: (1) 760 431 6948 or (800) 650 5115. www.hayhouse.com

Published and distributed in Australia by:
Hay House Australia Ltd, 18/36 Ralph St, Alexandria NSW 2015. Tel.: (61) 2 9669
4299; Fax: (61) 2 9669 4144. www.hayhouse.com.au

Published and distributed in the Republic of South Africa by:
Hay House SA (Pty), Ltd, PO Box 990, Witkoppen 2068. Tel./Fax: (27) 11 467
8904. www.hayhouse.co.za

Published and distributed in India by:
Hay House Publishers India, Muskaan Complex, Plot No.3, B-2, Vasant Kunj,
New Delhi – 110 070. Tel.: (91) 11 4176 1620; Fax: (91) 11 4176 1630.
www.hayhouse.co.in

Distributed in Canada by:
Raincoast, 9050 Shaughnessy St, Vancouver, BC V6P 6E5. Tel.: (1) 604 323 7100;
Fax: (1) 604 323 2600

Wayne Dyer's editor: Joanna Pyle
Cover design: Amy Rose Grigoriou • *Interior design:* Tricia Breidenthal
Interior photos: Courtesy of the author, except where noted

Margaret Runyon Castaneda's poem on p.119 is reprinted
with permission by C.J. Castaneda.

A catalogue record for this book is available from the British Library.

ISBN 978-1-84850-815-6

Printed and bound in Great Britain by TJ International, Padstow, Cornwall.

For the author of all things . . .

the I Am that I Am . . .

CONTENTS

"Guess now who holds thee?" —
"Death," I said. But, there,
The silver answer rang, —
"Not Death, but Love."

— ELIZABETH BARRETT BROWNING

THE BEGINNING

I have chosen to introduce this book by relating several experiences that have touched my life and reflect an appreciation of the essential messages you will read about in *Wishes Fulfilled*. These meaningful life events occurred during the creation of this book, and contain elements of synergy and synchronicity that I find very exciting and promising. I'm offering what I consider to be a program that guarantees you the ability to manifest into your life all that you desire, as long as what you desire remains aligned with your Source of being. In my everyday life, while I was writing the manuscript for this book, I was blessed to experience firsthand how this process works. I've chosen to share these miraculous occurrences in a very personal way.

As I begin my eighth decade here on planet Earth, I find myself looking back at the more notable influences in my life that seemed to just *show up*. From this distance, I can see the impact they had in reversing the ego-dominated direction my life was taking at those earlier times. When these exceptional signal events or people materialized in my past, I was unable, as most of us are unable at the time, to access the larger perspective of what was happening. Now, from this perspective of looking back and writing about how to live a wishes fulfilled life from a spiritual vantage point, I see those events as the pieces of a puzzle in a grand tapestry that is awe inspiring and very meaningful to me today.

Saint Francis

One person who *showed up* in my life was a man who lived back in the 13th century and is now known as Saint Francis of Assisi. I wasn't raised in any particular religious faith, probably because of being moved around to different foster homes during my childhood. I had no knowledge of Catholicism and was never exposed to any of the saints or their teachings. But for some mysterious (but much less mysterious today) reason, this monk who lived such an inspiring, Christ-conscious life was to be one of the truly most portentous and impactful beings to ever cross my life path.

Saint Francis's influence first appeared in my life in a large, beautifully framed print of the entire "Prayer of Saint Francis," which was given to me by someone at a lecture more than 25 years ago. The messages of the prayer resonated with me profoundly and I loved how it appeared, so I hung it in a hallway that led to my children's bedrooms. I must have walked by that prayer at least 10,000 times in the decade that it hung there. Often I'd pause, read a few lines, and contemplate the magic in the words: *Where there is hatred, let me sow love* and, *Where there is darkness, let me bring light.*

These words seemed more like a technology than a prayer. I loved thinking that hatred could grow into love, and darkness could be illuminated—not by asking God to do it, but by *being* love and light. It seemed to promise that we humans had the ability to literally change suffering and pain by transforming ourselves, and I enjoyed contemplating that achievement. But, from this vantage point, I can see that I wasn't yet ready to live Saint Francis's message, or even write it in the way that I've succeeded with this book.

Nevertheless, Francesco di Pietro di Bernardone (1181–1226) had come into my life, and his influence slowly began to engulf me as the years passed. I was persuaded to go to Assisi in the 1990s, and while there I felt in some unexplainable way I was home. I walked in the fields where Francesco walked; I meditated in the same little chapel where he prayed. I stood at his tomb mesmerized by the overwhelming feeling in my body that I was one with this man who had lived 800-plus years before my own birth.

I began to read about Francesco and was extremely moved by his burning desire to fulfill his own dharma alongside his determination not to let anything impede his dream. I too have felt that inner call to do the work I've done all these years. I too have had periods of being off the path, and always that inner voice bringing me back to writing and living each day—to my Divine mission.

About a decade ago I knew I was going to write a book titled *There's a Spiritual Solution to Every Problem,* but I was unclear about how to organize this undertaking. In a deep meditation I heard a strong voice say, *Base it on the "Prayer of Saint Francis" that hangs on the wall in your home.* It was a moment of such clarity and pure vision that I felt as if the book was already written. All I had to do was let myself "be an instrument of thy peace."

I returned again to Assisi and had another miraculous experience. I experienced a healing in my body that to this day remains a mystery to me and my medical doctor friends as well. (I related the story of this healing and my vision of Saint Francis in my movie, *The Shift.*) Once again this 13th-century monk had transformed my life by appearing to me and showing me that there are no limits to what can take place when one is living from a God-realized perspective.

I went on to write the book effortlessly, after taking copious notes on my second visit to Assisi. Furthermore, the subject matter of *There's a Spiritual Solution to Every Problem* became a public television special, and millions of people had the teachings of Saint Francis brought into their homes because of my calling to write about these profoundly life-transforming truths.

Years ago I found myself drawn to the fictional re-creation of the life of Saint Francis of Assisi, written by one of the greatest writers of our time, Nikos Kazantzakis. And to this day I still read from this amazing novel (*Saint Francis*) regularly and always find myself moved to tears and higher consciousness by its contents.

About a year ago I had another strong calling during a deep meditation to take a group of people to three spiritual cities in Europe: Lourdes in France; Medjugorje in Bosnia-Herzegovina; and, of course, Assisi in Italy. We called this journey "Experiencing the Miraculous," and 162 people from all over the globe signed on to visit these holy places where genuine miracles have taken place in the 13th, 19th, and 20th centuries. I offered a two-hour lecture in each of these remarkable places, and in our opening night gathering in Assisi, I told everyone that we were truly fulfilling the vision of Saint Francis. His objective was to bring Christ-conscious awareness to the entire world, one parish, one city, one country at a time. On this trip we had people from every continent, representing all age-groups from teenagers to octogenarians. All professions, all religious persuasions, all with the same ideas—to assist our world in being one that is populated by people who desire to "make me an instrument of thy peace," and thus create such a world from our deepest wishes desiring to be fulfilled.

On our second day in Assisi, on my third visit to this Divine city, all 162 people gathered in an ancient church built hundreds of years ago when Francesco lived there and began the Franciscan order. As my two-hour talk was winding down in this holy building, something happened to me that I have never experienced in almost four decades of public lectures. I felt something take over my body, and I was rendered speechless. I was doing a reading from Kazantzakis's *Saint Francis,* and at the end I simply froze. My body wouldn't move. I broke into almost furious sobbing, and the entire audience stood up and stretched out their hands to me in silence. Everyone knew that a truly metaphysical happening was transpiring. (The entire trip was filmed, including this and two other lectures. You can see it all for yourself if you so desire by viewing the *Experiencing the Miraculous* 4-DVD set that is produced by Hay House.)

Many photographs were taken of me speaking beneath a portrait of Jesus Christ in the church, and I have included one in the photo insert so that you might view the very large orb that made its appearance at that transfixing lecture in the holy church in Assisi. You will learn more about these orbs later in this book.

What I can say with certainty is that I once again felt in my body the power of Saint Francis. I experienced him, not only by his words and not only around me, but in me—*as me*—while speaking to those 162 people whom I feel were a catalytic group gathered for the purpose of fulfilling a collective dharma, originating in a thought in my imagination and now an active force for good in our world. Looking back at my life, at the events that brought Saint Francis into my life, it seems clear that I didn't recognize the significance of them at the time. I simply did what I felt called to do. And I must say that Francesco didn't just come into my life with an occasional message to prompt my own spiritual awakening, he actually took it over and changed the course that my life was taking at the time—he *lived* in me most of the time.

I am going to leave Saint Francis for a moment and relate the presence of another luminous being who arrived in my life about six years ago.

Lao-tzu

Back in 2005 I became reacquainted with the ancient spiritual text the Tao Te Ching, narrated some 2,500 years ago by the ancient Chinese master Lao-tzu. Some have called this small book containing 81 short verses the wisest book ever written. While I had a cursory awareness of the Tao, it was by no means a significant teaching in my life. Yet I noticed that at the age of 65 I kept reading and receiving messages from the Tao Te Ching, which translates loosely to *the book of living the virtue of the great way*.

I was familiar with some of the most quoted passages from the text and had even used them in my previously published books, but now in 2005 for some reason I seemed to be bombarded by them almost on a daily basis. In a restaurant several lines from the Tao appeared on the menu; I heard more quotations on a couple of TV shows; in a bookstore a translation was misplaced on a shelf right next to one of my books; a close friend told me a story of how he claimed to be a Taoist and the peace that it brought him; and someone I didn't know sent me a card deck containing each of the 81 brief verses, along with a drawing of Lao-tzu sitting on an ox, and the likeness seemed to speak to me like no drawing had before.

Then one morning in my meditation I felt a strong inner calling to read the entire Tao Te Ching, and I did so that very day. That evening I called my publisher and said I'd like to write a brief essay on each of the 81 verses on how to apply the ancient wisdom of Lao-tzu to today's modern world, and publish it as one volume titled *Change Your Thoughts—Change Your Life*. From that moment on, I began to feel the same relationship with Lao-tzu as I had been having with Saint Francis for the previous decade or so. I began to hear this man speaking to me in my early-morning meditations.

I mentioned this on my weekly radio show on HayHouse Radio.com, and an artist named Magali told me on the air that she'd channeled a likeness of Lao-tzu that she'd produced in a frenzy of automatic painting, and was sending to me. The painting arrived via overnight delivery, and I literally talked to this likeness for the entire year of 2006.

Each week I spent four and a half days studying, meditating, intellectualizing, and analyzing a verse of the Tao Te Ching. On the half day, after meditating with the painting of Lao-tzu, I simply let the words flow onto the page. I spent the entire year of 2006 communing with Lao-tzu, gazing at his portrait and watching how his eyes seemed to follow me as I moved about my writing space, and most significantly, listening and letting the words flow through my heart and onto the page.

My year of being steeped in the Tao Te Ching was truly life altering. I learned and practiced the essential messages of humility, living the mystery, contentment, simplicity, serenity, and finding God in nature rather than in an orthodoxy. Lao-tzu became my constant companion, and the Tao Te Ching not only guided me to a more enlightened way of life, it did so for millions of others as well. The Public Broadcasting Service (PBS) allowed me to present the essence of Lao-tzu's ancient messages on a pledge show that aired thousands of times, often in prime time, in every major market in the United States and Canada. Somehow in some mysterious way known only by the invisible Tao or the one Divine mind, I became an instrument for getting these powerful messages out to large numbers of people, 25 centuries after the passing of Lao-tzu.

Saint Francis and Lao-tzu and their teachings are still hugely consequential in my life every day. But more than being these momentous spiritual teachers, their appearances in my life have impacted countless others, including you as you embark on the reading of this book.

Brenda's Letter

I am now going to share a remarkable letter that I received a few days ago as I was preparing to write the opening pages of *Wishes Fulfilled*. Please read it with an open mind, and then allow me to explain the relevance it has for you as you begin reading this book.

> *Dear Dr. Wayne,*
>
> *Miracles happen. I feel compelled to share with you an experience I had very recently, because you were a part of the miracle that I experienced.*
>
> *Several months ago I heard about your "Experiencing the Miraculous" tour, and I knew that I had to be a part of it. Life for me is complicated right now as I go through a great big shift, so for me to work out the logistics of going on the European tour was likely to take a miracle, but I was open to anything. I stated my intention out loud. I said, "I intend to experience the miraculous with Dr. Wayne," and then I left it to God to come up with the hows.*
>
> *A few months passed and my situation was slow to change, so my trip was not booked. I continued to have faith and to know that I would experience the miraculous with you even if*

reality kept saying "not likely." In the beginning of April my busy schedule had me traveling with my 14-year-old daughter, Emily, to Kelowna, B.C., for her singing festival. It is an eight-hour drive from where I live, but she is very passionate about opera, so giving her the opportunity to go to Kelowna to work with some experts was certainly my pleasure. My parents happen to live there, too, so I called them to say we were coming.

I talked to Mom for a few minutes, told her when we would be arriving, and chatted about this and that when I heard Dad mumbling something in the background. Mom interpreted for me: "Your Dad says Dr. Wayne Dyer will be in Vernon Tuesday night if you want to go see him." Well, after I picked the phone (and myself) off of the floor, I asked Dad if he would be my date, and I went online and bought tickets. Needless to say, I was thrilled that God would be so kind as to bring you to me instead of getting me to Europe.

The night of your lecture came, and I eagerly sat in the 14th row. When you walked onstage and started to talk, something weird happened. It had happened once before when I saw a young boy sing "Ave Maria," and a huge halo of light appeared around him. At first I had thought I was getting a migraine, but the light was only around the young boy. That same light was surrounding you. No matter where you moved on the stage, the light followed you, and only you. I thought it might be the stage lights or the ambient atmosphere in the arena, but there was no halo around the lady who introduced you.

Then something even stranger happened. Dr. Wayne, you were talking about Saint Francis and before my very eyes, you transformed. Your body was clad in a long robe and your features transformed so that you <u>were</u> Saint Francis of Assisi. It lasted for only a moment, but it was powerful, emotional, and very, very real.

But then something even stranger happened. You began to talk about Lao-tzu, and you transformed into him! A long braid tailed down your back, and I could see your face completely transform into Lao-tzu. Again, it only lasted for a moment, but the experience will last with me forever.

At intermission, Dad went to the restroom and I stood up to stretch my legs (and dry my eyes). I felt a warm hand fill mine and I looked down to see a little lady, very old and with a wonderful smile, and she was urging me to sit beside her. I sat, and she stared straight into my eyes. She told me that she kept staring at me because I was glowing with light and she felt like she was watching an angel. I was transfixed by her eyes, thinking that I knew her somehow because I recognized her twinkly green eyes. She and I talked, at times saying the same thing at the same time. Things like "We are all the same" and "There is only love" and other deeply spiritual things. It felt like a dream, and before we knew it you were onstage again, creating your magic. I decided I needed to perpetuate contact with her and would get her name and number after the show. Despite my good intentions, when the show ended and we got up to leave, she had disappeared. This surprised me because she had been sitting two seats away from me and I never saw her leave.

Dad and I left, and as I was backing the car up in the parking lot I caught sight of my own eyes in the rearview mirror. And that's when I realized where I had seen those twinkly green eyes before.

Impossible? Maybe . . . not. I have no explanation for any of the things I experienced that night, but every day I give thanks that I was able to "experience the miraculous" with Dr. Wayne in such a unique and lovely way.

Namaste,
Brenda Babinski

If you are wondering about her "twinkly green eyes" reference, it makes perfect sense to me because I readily recall Marcelene, the mother of seven of my children, telling me of her experience giving birth to her firstborn son, Shane. In the hospital she was struggling in labor and didn't wish to use anesthesia. A nurse with distinct red hair came to her side, wiped her brow, spoke soothingly and lovingly to her of how to breathe, and stayed with her throughout the entire birth process. When she inquired the next day about this wonderfully helpful nurse and how she could properly thank her, she was told that no one of that description had ever worked in that hospital. Angelic guidance—perhaps. And Brenda's encounter with her very old little lady may also have been an encounter with her highest self (see Chapter Three).

I include Brenda's letter here in the beginning to give you a sense of what is possible when you begin to assume the feeling of a wish fulfilled, as I detail in Chapter Six. My first thought upon reading Brenda's words came directly from my ego, which declared, *You were probably Lao-tzu and then Saint Francis in two of your previous lives, and why not. Look how important you are and all that you are doing to make this a more spiritually awakened place.* Then I talked by telephone with author Anita Moorjani in Hong Kong and read her the letter, and she quickly put my ego-driven thoughts to rest. She said that her experience of being on the "other side" was perfectly clear on one thing: Everything is happening at once. There is no past or future, only one and only now. And that the closest she could come to this idea was that these are all parallel lives.

Now I know how perplexing it is to contemplate this idea of no past, no future, and no linear consciousness, especially since the brain (which is the only thing we have to do this contemplating with) is in a body that is linear and did have a beginning and will have an end. It is simply one of the great mysteries, this idea of everything happening at once, yet in my dream state and occasionally in deep meditation I have had a glimpse of this nonlinearity. I urge you to read Anita's book, *Dying to Be Me,* to gain perhaps a bit more understanding of how the now/oneness appeared to her as she embarked upon her healing journey away from a certain death prognosis.

As you read *Wishes Fulfilled* I encourage you to take notice of the importance of being able to *feel* in your body what you desire to manifest. Pay particular attention to what it means to *know* within that you are truly a Divine being here in the material world of ours on Earth. I repeatedly emphasize, in the pages that follow, the importance of your imagination in creating a wishes fulfilled life. But your imagination is strictly a domain that's controlled by your thinking processes. Once you place a thought into your imagination about who you want to become, I encourage you to live from that end, as if it had already materialized into the physical realm.

And this is precisely what I have been doing with the teachings of both Saint Francis and Lao-tzu for many years: living their messages intellectually; writing about them, lecturing on them, analyzing them, interpreting them—all in my imagination. But now at this time in my life, I have gone beyond my intellect when it comes to the teachings of these Divine masters. When I appeared onstage that evening in Vernon, B.C., and when I spoke to that audience in Assisi and felt myself overwhelmed by the presence of Saint Francis, I was *feeling* them in my body, living their messages as if they were me—or, in other words, *assuming the feeling of the wish to know their truths as already fulfilled.* And when you are able to passionately feel whatever it is that you wish to have or become, as long as it is aligned with your highest self—that is, God—you become it and it becomes you.

When I teach these profound messages, they are way beyond an intellectual exercise. I feel them, and this is what Brenda Babinski observed in those fleeting moments while I was onstage. Imagine it; live as if it were your reality; allow no detractors; but, most important, assume the feeling of it, and you will merge with it and it will merge with you so that it is no longer a duality—it is you becoming one with what you desire.

That same evening Brenda came to see me, as I sat onstage and signed books, the entire hockey arena was filled with orbs as if to confirm the convergence of the truths of both Saint Francis and Lao-tzu as I assumed the feeling of these spiritual truths in the core of my being. (See photo insert.) Those orbs also appeared in photographs at the church in Assisi where I felt in my body the presence of Saint Francis as I stood and spoke where he had lived and spoken. (Again, see photo insert.) I do not believe that my being seen by an audience member as actually transforming into these great teachers is an indication that I might have lived as them many centuries ago. I know that when you begin to go beyond the intellect and feel the presence of what you most desire as an already present fact, and live from it with unabated passion, you merge into it, and come to know the truth that the laws of the material world do not apply in the presence of the God-realized.

Nicollette

I have chosen to relate one additional story here in the beginning of *Wishes Fulfilled* that brings home the most salient feature of this book. That is, that there exists within all of us a Divine spark, called the *I am that I am*, and when it is kindled and nourished, it is capable of miracle-making at an astonishing level.

In May of 2011 I met a group of women, including a mother and her 20-year-old daughter, while on a walk along the oceanfront on Maui. Linda, the mom, recognized me, and we began a brief conversation. As I looked at her daughter, Nicollette, it was obvious that she was suffering from some kind of facial paralysis that had distorted her features—the muscle activity in the entire left side of her face appeared to be frozen. Something motivated me to reach out and touch her face and ask her what was happening. And then began a saga that I have chosen, with permission from both of them, to relate here in this book to give you a sampling of what is possible when we use the inherent power that is a part of our very essence—called the *I am* presence—for the fulfillment of our Divinely aligned wishes.

I felt called to invite the entire group of women into my home and to talk to Nicollette about the wishes fulfilled teachings that I was channeling and writing about each and every day, and had been for several months. I spent an hour or so with Nicollette while her mother, grandmother, and two of Linda's friends stayed in the background. During this time I felt in my body that something stupefying and mystical was energizing not only me but the entire room.

At the end of our time together, I insisted that Nicollette spend an hour with my friend Kate MacKinnon, a craniosacral therapist who was visiting and offering me CST treatments. I had set up an appointment for myself with Kate for the following day. I gave my appointment to Nicollette, and what follows are two descriptions of the event that transpired. The first is Linda's letter to Kate about her understanding of the entire experience.

> Hi Kate,
>
> I wanted to tell you that before Hawaii, Nicollette did not know of Wayne Dyer at all. She is a university student consumed with classes, assignments, work, and parties and has never been to his lectures or read his books. She still knows very little of him other than she is now reading The Power of Intention.
>
> On Saturday I arrived in Hawaii with my husband, Gord, and son, Jason. Nicollette called me from Victoria, B.C., the next day. She said she had experienced a weird headache the night before, and now her face was going numb on the left side. She was having difficulty smiling on one side and was worried. She sent a picture of herself from her phone and we told her to go to the emergency room now and get it looked at, for it may be a stroke or something! Nicollette didn't want to go because she said she had too much schoolwork to do, had final exams to study for, and didn't feel well enough to go. I insisted we needed a professional assessment. She went and was triaged immediately through and given a battery of tests.
>
> She called me about an hour later and said she was diagnosed with a very severe case of Bell's palsy—cause unknown. They had theories of causes, but didn't see the other physical effects of these causes and so the doctors were stumped by her condition. She was given prophylactic antiviral medication and

13

high doses of prednisone. It not being a life-threatening condition, they said, "Sorry, this is all we can do—time will tell," and she was sent home.

Nicollette was beside herself with grief. She called us and was so-o-o upset. We suggested that if the doctors said it was okay, then she would come to Hawaii or I'd fly home to be with her. She spent the next two days seeing different physicians making sure she could travel. She arrived in Hawaii on Tuesday.

We could see that her paralysis was worse when she arrived —it was definitely progressing. It worsened for several days thereafter. I was in contact with our doctor at home and sent him another picture of Nicollette in full paralysis. He told me that based on what he saw in the photo, it was a severe case. He told us to be prepared that there's a strong possibility that she may only partially recover from this or . . . perhaps not at all! Furthermore, this type of palsy (Ramsay Hunt) can be quite painful and may have nasty side effects from the nerve damage that has been done.

At the doctor's request, we went to the local drugstore and purchased full-coverage eye patches and eye lubrications so her left eye would not ulcerate, as it was no longer closing.

A week or so passed, paralysis continued, no movement, nor any taste sensation on her left side of her tongue. Her left eyebrow nerves were blown out, eye couldn't close, nostril and mouth affected as well. She was having difficulty chewing. Nicollette was in a state of stress, distress, and shooting pain.

The universe intervenes—we meet Dr. Wayne Dyer on the promenade.

We spent about an hour with Wayne in his condo. Wayne was totally focused on Nicollette's state of mind and on healing. She was wanting to heal right now, being told she has the power to heal, but didn't know how to get to the place to tap into that healing. Wayne put his hands on her face and spoke to her over and over again, the same words until she got it— _I am paralysis-free!_ My girlfriends in the background were crying, my mother awestruck . . . as we were leaving his condo, Wayne insisted that Nicollette must, simply must, have a session with his CST therapist the next day. Since time was an issue, he gave his appointment to Nicollette. He made the arrangements.

Nicollette came into the therapy session with much gratitude and the new thinking that she will be healed. But she said that one of her barriers to healing was that she couldn't get to a place of completely "letting go and letting God" because she was in fight-or-flight mode. "How can I get to a state of physical relaxation and heal when I don't know how to relax my body?"

I recall she expressed these concerns to you and you understood what she was saying. You asked her (as Wayne had asked her, too) what was going on in her life before this had happened. She said, "Nothing. Everything's fine. I was studying for my final exams in economics and computer science, and at the same time I needed to create a painting for my art class and write an essay on it. My roommate is moving out and also I'm anxiously waiting to find out if I'm going to be accepted to McGill University in Montreal. Lots on my plate, but I am handling it."

You said to her, "Nicollette, that isn't nothing. That is a lot of something. We see here how the mind and mind-filled stress can affect the body. This is the mind/body connection, or rather _dis_connection."

Once we got back to Vancouver, Nicollette and I met with our family doctor. He told my daughter that this was indeed a "very moderate" case. To translate, by his expression and from what he had told me over the phone in Hawaii, it was actually severe. Nicollette knew what he meant. She knew it was severe, but it didn't bother her because as far as she was concerned, she was healing. Our family doctor then went on to provide statistics of different levels of recovery and to prepare us that this type of paralysis can take two years or more to come back from, if you do come back. We were to schedule another appointment in four weeks where Nicollette would be referred to a neurologist.

I can't say for sure when she actually had visible improvement, for she went back almost immediately to the University of Victoria to make up all the work that she had missed while in Hawaii. She went back with the confidence of simply moving forward. I was surprised that she was leaving us and getting right back into her university life after what our family doctor had said, and given that she was still paralyzed.

No matter what I thought or what I said, in true Nicollette conviction, she continued to tell me, "Mom, you don't get it! Didn't you hear what Wayne said? I am healed and paralysis-free. Didn't you hear me say that, too? What part of that don't you understand? I am healed—it's just that you and everybody else in this world can't see it yet!"

Four weeks later she is paralysis-free.

Namaste,

Linda

The words *I am healed* and *I am paralysis-free* that Nicollette spoke, even though the physical evidence strongly indicated otherwise, may sound strange or even absurd to you as you read this. But I assure you they will make sense as you read *Wishes Fulfilled*.

The second description is Nicollette's recollection in a letter to the craniosacral therapist, Kate MacKinnon.

Hi Kate,

Thank you so much for letting my mom know about Dr. Dyer's radio show today. My family and I listened to it this evening, and I am so grateful that you made it possible for all of us to hear those wonderful things. This is truly, and has been, an amazing experience. I can't thank you enough for all that you have done.

Initially, at the time of my diagnosis with Bell's palsy on the first day of spring, I just could not move the left side of my bottom lip as much as I could the right side. Four days later I couldn't move the entire left side of my face at all; I couldn't even close my left eye and had to tape it shut every night. I could see my paralysis getting worse every day no matter how

16

much I thought it would get better. I came to the conclusion that I had no control over the left side of my face. I was told that I might not ever recover from this, and if I do it could take years. I became miserable. I felt broken. I was suffering.

I met Dr. Dyer the day before I was leaving Maui. I didn't know who he was, or what he is about. After Dr. Dyer learned of my condition, he put his hand over my face and introduced the idea that I have the power to heal myself. All I have to do is think about how I feel when I am paralysis-free. I thought about a friend taking a picture of me a year ago and me having no paralysis—I was smiling. It was then explained that the physical is a representation of what starts out in the mind, in my imagination, of what I want to be physically. Manifestation and healing begin here. I began to think that if I changed my thought process and thought only of connecting myself with the knowing that I am paralysis-free, eventually, the physical will reflect my new mind-set. Dr. Dyer then said that he highly recommended I have a session with you, and he gave me your number. I called you, and with the generosity and kindness of Dr. Dyer, I had a session with you the next day.

Right after meeting Dr. Dyer, I had difficulty trying to connect to the thought of being paralysis-free because it was so prominent to me in everything I did. I couldn't chew properly, taste very well, or pronounce some words without feeling uncomfortable. My eye was always dry during the day, and at night I had to tape it shut after putting this lube in it.

I also had so much on my mind. I had two finals in one week's time worth more than 60 percent of my grade, and I had to maintain a certain GPA to stay in my program at the University of Victoria and to still have a good chance of getting into McGill University. In addition, I had to figure out living accommodations in three weeks. I had so much to think about, and I felt so uncomfortable in everything I did because of my paralysis. I was holding on to the stress of it all, still focusing on the Bell's palsy. I didn't want it to have a negative impact on my life—but it was. The next day I had a session with you.

You asked what was going on in my life before this happened. I said, "Nothing. Everything was fine." I felt I was doing well on my time management with my studies, keeping up with my assignments in economics, computer science, and art class. My roommate was moving out, and I was also. I was anxiously waiting to find out if I was going to be accepted to McGill University. I knew it seemed like a lot, but I didn't feel the stress of it. I even remember thinking that I should feel more stressed out than I did.

You said to me, "Nicollette, that isn't nothing. That is a lot of something. We see here how stress hurts the body. This is the mind/body connection or more like <u>dis</u>connection."

I lay down and the healing began. You started by putting your hands on my ankles. You were asking my mom some questions about where we are from, etc. It made me feel more comfortable, as this was something I had never heard of or even imagined I would be doing. I didn't know how to think of the situation. So I started thinking about how I could make this session as beneficial as possible. I thought about what Dr. Dyer had said to me the day before and what I had read in Anita Moorjani's near-death-experience article. I constantly told myself, "I am paralysis-free," and thought about the picture of me a year ago, smiling.

You asked me if I like the ocean, and I replied, "Yes." You told me to listen to the sound of the waves crashing against the sand on the shore. I remember hearing the calming sound of the waves and looking up at the white ceiling. Looking at the ceiling, it was almost as if my body was now numb and I could no longer feel your hands, which were now touching my legs. When you got to my rib cage on my left side, you asked me if I had stomach pains. I explained that I have had extreme pain in the stomach region after every time I ate something, but I thought it was caused by the medication I had to take for my Bell's palsy. However, I finished my medication a week ago, and I am still having pain there. You focused around my stomach and rib cage. I was looking up at the ceiling. I began to feel pressure right underneath my rib cage, but was unsure if I should say something. Then you said, "If you feel any pressure anywhere, let me know."

Immediately I felt more pressure in that spot, so I said so. I was staring at the ceiling and it began to change colors. You asked me if the pain was a shape what shape would it be, and what color. I said it would be an oval and yellow. You asked if this oval had a name. Nothing came to me. Therefore, you said we can call it yellow oval, and asked me if this oval is working with me. I felt like it was working against me and said that. You said, "That's no good." And I remember agreeing in my thoughts.

You told me to talk to this yellow oval and ask if we can work together. So I did just that. Then, seconds later, I felt it gone. Almost as if the oval had burst into a million pieces floating all over my body and I became one with it. I felt a state of complete relaxation. After that experience I would say that you helped me realize this control I have over my body. You helped me jump-start the communication between my mind and my body. I was introduced to the notion of how my mind and my body are one.

I remember hearing the waves and repeatedly telling myself, "I am paralysis-free." You got to my head. I felt your fingers right at the top of my spine, at the top of my neck. You kept your hands there for a while it seemed. Then, I felt my lower back touch the surface of what I was lying on. I felt as if what was making me feel so uncomfortable all this time had left my body. I took a deep breath, and I vividly remember the air going in so easily. I felt connected to my body as I could feel the air going in and out so freely.

You then focused on the left side of my mouth and kept your fingers on the bottom of my upper left molars for a few minutes. Then you touched the left side of my face. I felt relaxed, and I had the picture of me smiling in my mind. I opened myself up to the notion that you are going to be the catalyst in my healing process. You asked me for a word that will help me heal, and what color it would need. I got the word "feel" and the color of light blue and I repeated them to you.

You asked me to feel your hand on my face, and imagine my face as a sponge absorbing your energy. I pictured this light blue sponge contracting. I did feel your hand on my face. I saw the sponge in my mind, and I told myself that "I am paralysis-free." I was in a state of complete relaxation picturing this sponge as I felt your hand, and heard the waves of the ocean. I felt one with my body, that I had control of my body, and that I was smiling paralysis-free.

You had your hand on my face for what seemed to be about five minutes. However, my concept of time during that session could be incorrect. Then you lifted your hand off my face and I opened my eyes. You were looking down at me and asked me how I felt. I can't remember my response, although I felt relaxed, and aware of what was going on in and around my body. I remember you telling me that I grind my teeth on my left side of my mouth, and asked me if something happened to my forehead (which I banged on the roof of my car the day before coming to Hawaii, as I told you later). I remember you telling me that whatever it is I would normally do to relax I need to do more of because that is when the healing takes place.

The session overall is a blur other than those feelings I described above. At the end, I almost expected to be able to physically smile paralysis-free, but when I couldn't, I was a little disappointed. Then within a matter of minutes after that thought of disappointment had entered my mind, other thoughts poured in—healing thoughts. After putting on the shoes I took off before the session, I noticed a weird feeling in my body—a physical feeling—something had definitely changed. I felt a sense of peace. I knew my suffering was over. I physically was no longer uncomfortable. I felt excited and filled with energy. I knew I was healing—I knew it.

Over the next few weeks, I continued to think about what you had said about how the healing takes place in relaxation. So, whenever I felt my senses speaking to me, convincing me that I still have a severe case of facial paralysis (like for ex-ample when I couldn't pronounce some words properly when speaking to my mom right after the session), I thought of the light blue sponge, and the feeling of your hand on my face. Every time I think of that sponge I am brought back to that place of total relaxation, with the suffering and uncomfortable feelings suddenly lifted from my body. I hear the sound of the waves overpower what my senses tell me, and all that is left in my mind is that picture of me smiling. When I left Maui I had an overwhelming feeling and image of healing. I am paralysis-free, I am paralysis-free, I am paralysis-free!

Nicollette

I was scheduled to give an evening lecture in Canada at the Jubilee Auditorium in Calgary, Alberta, some ten weeks after my first and only encounter with Nicollette. Linda had called me to re-port that her daughter was completely paralysis-free, and that this experience had completely turned her entire life mission around.

I called Nicollette, and she excitedly told me how great she felt to have learned at the age of 20 that she had this amazing *I am* presence within her and that she wanted to tell everyone she encountered about this profound discovery. I invited her and her mom to come to Calgary and share her experience with the sev-eral thousand people I would be speaking to. And indeed she did.

In only a few moments Nicollette transfixed the audience, giv-ing real-world, 3-D evidence of all that I was lecturing about that evening. As she left the stage to a standing ovation, she handed me a card with two photos imprinted on it. (See photo insert.) In the photo of the three of us in Hawaii (Nicollette, Linda, and me), the left side of her face is paralyzed. In the other photo, Nicollette is smiling in a beautiful dress, paralysis-free—with a distinct orb at her left shoulder! The caption on the card says: *A Wish Fulfilled, Love, Nicollette and Linda.*

As you continue reading this book, which has been such a miraculous journey for me, know that I take no credit for any of it. I'm reminded of the 1977 film *Oh, God!* with George Burns as

God saying something to the effect that if you want a miracle, you should try to make a fish from scratch. Only the *I am* presence is so equipped.

I give full credit to that presence and urge you to know that it is yours to access as well. Do it—from scratch!

Sending love,
Wayne Dyer

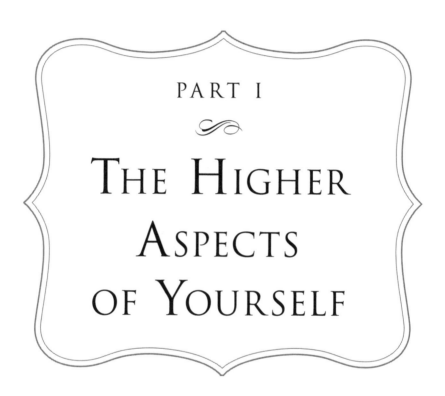

PART I

THE HIGHER ASPECTS OF YOURSELF

"Part of me suspects I'm a loser, and part of me thinks I'm God Almighty."

— JOHN LENNON

CHANGING
YOUR CONCEPT
OF YOURSELF

"Health, wealth, beauty, and genius are not created;
they are only manifested by the arrangement of your mind—
that is, by your concept of yourself, and your concept of
yourself is all that you accept and consent to as true."[1]

—NEVILLE

There's a level of awareness available to you that you are probably unfamiliar with. It extends upward and transcends the ordinary level of consciousness that you're most accustomed to. At this
higher plane of existence, which you and every human being who
has ever lived can access at will, the fulfillment of wishes is not
only probable—it is guaranteed. This chapter is simply a preparation for entering into that realm wherein you have much more say
over what comes into your life than you might have envisioned.

After 18 months in relative seclusion, studying, meditating,
and literally experiencing what it's like to live in this miraculous plane of existence beyond anything that might be labeled

"ordinary" or "normal," I've undertaken this joyous task of writing about having wishes fulfilled. I've seen firsthand how virtually every wish or desire I've placed my attention on has transformed from a mental thought into an objective fact.

However, I'm not proposing memorizing an esoteric formula leading to a theoretical nirvana. My emphasis throughout this book is that manifestation is *real* and that it occurs when you make a specific decision to change your mind about who you are and what is possible for you to achieve within these parentheses in eternity called *your life.*

I'm inviting you to be receptive to a radical new idea about yourself. It's radical because ever since you left your mother's womb, you've been subjected to cultural conditioning designed to help you be content with living a "normal life" at the level of ordinary consciousness, which generally means accepting whatever life hands you. In many ways you've been programmed to believe that you do not possess the wisdom or ability to manifest the fulfillment of your wishes and desires.

I am saying as clearly as I know how to say it in these opening pages: *There's a plane of awareness that you can opt to live at, wherein you can, if you are willing to change your concept of yourself as an ordinary being, find yourself fulfilling any and all wishes that you have for yourself.* Throughout this book I'll explore with you what I've studied, learned, internalized, practiced, and, yes, *lived* regarding the powers of manifestation. It begins with changing your concept of yourself.

I would like to offer a few words on these two concepts of ordinary and extraordinary.

Ordinary is, well, so ordinary. It means that you do all of the things that your culture and your family have programmed you to do. It implies that you fit in, study hard, follow the rules, take care of your obligations, fill out the forms, pay your taxes, get a job, and do what every law-abiding citizen does; and then you retire, play with your grandchildren, and ultimately die. I want to emphasize that there is absolutely nothing wrong with this scenario—it is perfectly fine—but if it were completely acceptable for you, you wouldn't be reading this book.

Extraordinary encompasses most of ordinary, since we all live in the same physical world. There will be forms to fill out, rules that demand our obedience, bills to pay, and family obligations to attend to. But extraordinary consciousness is associated with your soul, that invisible, boundaryless energy that looks out from behind your eyeballs and has very different interests than your ordinary self does.

The ideal of your soul, the thing that it yearns for, is not more knowledge. It is not interested in comparison, nor winning, nor light, nor ownership, nor even happiness. The ideal of your soul is space, expansion, and immensity, and the one thing it needs more than anything else is to be free to expand, to reach out and to embrace the infinite. Why? Because your soul is infinity itself. It has no restrictions or limitations—it resists being fenced in— and when you attempt to contain it with rules and obligations, it is miserable.

Your invisible self is extraordinary because it is a fragment of the universal soul, which is infinite. The part of you that knows you have greatness, and is stirred by the idea of you expanding and removing any and all limitations, is what I am addressing here in *Wishes Fulfilled*. This is your new self-concept, one that is inspired by your soul.

So let's take a look at this idea and then examine what you need to do in order to make your self-concept congruent with how you want to live your life, and the powerful role you can begin to assume as a co-fulfiller of all of your rational/sensible wishes and desires.

What Is Your Self-Concept?

Simply put, your concept of yourself is everything that you believe to be true. And everything that you believe to be true about yourself has landed you precisely where you live and breathe every day of your life. Your beliefs about yourself are like the ingredients in a recipe that you use to create your self-concept. Those ingredients or beliefs fall into two specific categories: *your outer self-concept* and *your inner self-concept.*

Your Outer Self-Concept

These ingredients include everything you accept as truth concerning what the physical you is capable of. There's probably a certain amount of intellectual acumen that you agree is necessary to your outer self-concept. Smart, perhaps, but not really a genius—more capable in some areas than others, such as technological knowledge. Maybe you add a measure of writing ability, but detect more fluency with numbers and mathematical problem solving than your ability to write prose. Your beliefs about your outer self may be well seasoned and strong in some areas and almost hopelessly incapacitated or weak in others. You very likely have a conceptual framework of just how smart you are and have carried that belief with you since you were a youngster in elementary school.

Your outer concept of yourself includes everything you believe about your innate and learned talents and abilities. Your beliefs about your clumsiness, coordination, athleticism, and musical and artistic talents are a partial list of the ingredients that comprise the recipe of you. These descriptors also apply to everything else about your outer self. Your outer self-concept includes how you view yourself in relationship to health: your immunity to, or inclination toward, illnesses of all descriptions. You know if you are prone to being overweight or addicted to various substances such as sugar, caffeine, fat, meat, dairy, and the like. You define yourself as prone to catching colds or immune to such things, likely to gain weight, inclined toward skin rashes, or predisposed to low energy or high sleep requirements.

The point is that your outer self-concept comprises essentially everything that you believe your body is capable or incapable of. Given a true/false test on yourself, you'd be able to say with certainty, *Yes, these things are true about me.* They are the beliefs—the ingredients—that you use to create you.

In addition to your intellect, talents, and physical body traits, you spice up your outer self-conception with your personality traits. You know if you're assertive or shy, loud or quiet, pushy or obsequious, fearful or courageous, daring or frightened—and this is only a partial list of personality descriptors or spices. These individual qualities are interpreted as truisms defining yourself and how you function socially.

I could continue detailing all of the other ingredients that go into making your outer self-concept, but I've chosen to keep this book short, succinct, and to the point. At this point I'm simply encouraging you to recognize that your self-concept contains a myriad of self-descriptors regarding this thing that you call your physical body, and that you probably regard them as absolute truth.

Your Inner Self-Concept

This category can be pretty difficult to achieve in optimal proportions in our culture. Your inner self-concept involves your beliefs about the invisible energy and intelligence that is the most significant portion of your being. I've often referred to your inner world as "the ghost in the machine." The machine in my conceptualization is your body and its five senses, as well as all of the physical components that make up your body. The tissue, bones, rivers of fluids, organs, teeth, brain, and everything else are all the machine. And within this machine is an invisible *I* that you call *mind* or *spirit* comprised of thoughts that direct the machine.

I once had a conversation with a neurosurgeon who was disputing the presence of this invisible world by saying that he'd cut into thousands of bodies and had never seen a soul. I remember his awkward look when I asked him if he'd ever seen a thought while he was poking around inside a brain.

Obviously there's an invisible inner as well as an outer part of your being. You have a conceptualization of yourself that involves this formless invisible portion of your being, and you have a pretty specific idea about just how far this inner portion of yourself can take you. You may believe that your thinking apparatus is pretty phenomenal, though not understanding exactly what it is—inside or surrounding you—that allows you to scratch your forehead, or pick up a pencil, or move your feet on a dance floor, or any of the infinite commands that your mind is capable of directing all day, every day, and for as long as you are alive.

You also have a self-concept about what your inner energetic ghost *cannot* do. Is it capable of *thinking* itself out of a serious disease, or is that just a lot of nonsense? Can your invisible intelligence, your imagination, perform feats of alchemy? Does your self-concept contain the power to perform great—or even magical —acts of transformation?

Your self-concept is a blend of your beliefs regarding your connection to a higher power. You believe something about the existence or nonexistence of God. You have various points of view about how far faith can carry you. Whether or not there is anything within you that you can or cannot rely on to perform mystical or miraculous things is seasoned by your beliefs. You have acquired specific beliefs concerning the power of your mind. You're generally confident that you can rely on your invisibleness to do the ordinary things in life such as remember an unseen list of items stored somewhere in your memory, and run errands on your way home from work. But what do your beliefs cook up about your ability to create *miracles?* Is healing your body, or manifesting a long-desired soul mate, an ingredient in your self-concept?

Take a moment to examine that unseen list stored away in your mind. Ask yourself, *Where is it? How did I put it there? Where is the place I'm calling "there"? What powers am I using to recall it? Where do these powers come from?* This is the list of ingredients that you use to create your inner self-concept. You might then want to open up to there being other beliefs or ingredients that you want to include, and contemplate other ways to season your life.

The fact is that an invisible list involves a catalog of inexplicable miracles that you take for granted every day. Your inner self-concept tells you what you believe your mind is capable of, and what it's incapable of as well. You know your mind, that invisible ghost in the machine, is unfathomable. But you also *know* that there are certain limits to what it can do.

Have you ever considered how you are creating your life with this inner self-concept's list of ingredients? If it seems interesting to consider some changes, read on.

Changing Your Concept of Yourself

If you would like to become a person who has the capacity to have all of your wishes fulfilled, it will be necessary for you to move to that higher plane of existence where you are a co-creator of your life. This means that you'll need to undertake what is often presumed to be the difficult task of changing your concept of yourself.

Recall that your concept of yourself is everything that you believe to be true about your inner and outer self. Those beliefs have created the life you're now living—at what I call an ordinary level of awareness. To move into the extraordinary space that I'm writing about in this book requires you to change what you believe is true. This can be a laborious project and an undertaking that, in my experience, few people are eager or willing to take on. I am writing this book to give you some very specific guidance and help in doing just that.

I'll be quoting a man by the name of Neville Goddard, who wrote and spoke to large audiences in America under the solitary name of Neville. A popular speaker on metaphysical themes from the late '30s until his death in 1972, Neville authored ten books in which he captured the sheer logic of creative mind principles. His work has impacted me in a very profound way; in fact, he's been a great mentor to me in the past few years.

31

Neville writes in a style that many might find strenuous to interpret, yet I find his teaching congruent with much of my earlier writing on manifestation and co-creation. That being said, Neville's teachings add a dimension that I hadn't really contemplated in depth until now. While studying his book *The Power of Awareness,* I began blending many of Neville's teachings with other great thinkers' ideas, revising and refining his unique personal theology into a practice that feels to me is meant for the world we inhabit today.

After giving each of my eight children a copy of *The Power of Awareness,* they individually expressed a variation of this: "I love his ideas, Dad, but I have to read each paragraph over and over and stop to think about what he's saying. I know he's right and it makes perfect sense, but I need it explained more—in words that I can understand and apply." Their comments fueled my desire to share many of Neville's ideas, most of which are compatible with my own, and create a synthesis addressing the power you have to fulfill your 21st-century wishes.

I want to share with you my sense of what this great teacher's ideas can do for you, as they have done for me. I know that Neville wouldn't mind because he freely allowed students and audience members to tape his talks without charge. His tapes continue to informally spread his message today, and I've listened to them while preparing to write this book. I feel as a kindred spirit to Neville, since I too have had the same policy during my entire speaking career, and have been immersed in the same kinds of spiritual inquiry as this great teacher who preceded me by a single generation.

Here is what Neville had to say regarding changing your self-concept in order to elevate your life: "If you refuse to assume the responsibility of the incarnation of a new and higher concept of yourself, then you *reject the means, the only means, whereby your redemption—that is, the attainment of your ideal—can be effected.*"[2]

Get this clearly in your head in this first chapter: *A higher concept of yourself involves taking on new truths and shedding your old views of what you can achieve. This is the only way you can achieve your desires.* That is the reason I'm stressing this early in this book. You must begin by replacing your old set of truths with a belief in the existence of a higher self within you. This is something that you may not have contemplated at an earlier time in your life.

Your concept of yourself that includes any limitations can be revised by you, and only by you. Nothing I say or write will do that for you. I have done it for myself and can *assist* you along this path, but it is your decision to change that creates the possibility of change within you. A new and higher concept of yourself may be shocking and perhaps even be rejected by you, depending on the amount of conditioning you have absorbed throughout your life. That is for you to ponder and contemplate in the next two chapters. At this point, simply allow yourself to imagine that you can create a new and higher concept of yourself. Resistance is what will almost immediately appear for most people, and I encourage you to recognize the resistance within yourself.

Overcoming Resistance

Making the transition from the level of ordinary consciousness to the level of superconsciousness involves a fundamental renewal—a dramatic change of personality. Very few are prepared to commit to this fulfillment of their Divine purpose. What I'm inviting you to do, if you wish to be truly fulfilled, is to overcome your resistance to including *all that you are* in your earthly life. You have the ability to enter higher regions so as to consciously fulfill your highest desires here, now, for the greater benefit of all. This is akin to doing a somersault and landing in a new reality— a reality in which all things are possible, a reality where you no longer identify yourself with all of those cultural memes and mind viruses that were programmed into you as a young person, preparing you for an ordinary life.

You begin this exciting adventure of changing your concept of yourself by being willing to die to your present self. That's right, by relinquishing your personal history as the arbiter of your life, you cease to resist your fuller potential. You simply no longer choose to form your identity on the basis of what you've been taught. Remind yourself that everything you've believed to be true has brought you to this point where you want to *explore* rather than *resist* your higher powers.

Years ago while reading Napoleon Hill's *Think and Grow Rich,* I recall him saying that there's one distinguishing characteristic of those who live life at a higher level with a richness that's not just about monetary gain. It is that these unique and rare individuals have a burning desire to succeed. Now, *a burning desire* is much different from a regular wish or desire because it burns inside—once ignited, it never goes out, regardless of what transpires. This is a quality that I know well. Often it feels like an obsession . . . and I have been labeled obsessive many times in my lifetime. Yet it hasn't been a curse, because it has always served me in the fulfillment of whatever yearning I felt inside of me. I often think of it as an inner candle flame that never even flickers, though the worst goes before me. All transformation begins with an intense burning desire to be transformed.

An inner knowing, along with a burning desire, is the prerequisite for becoming a person capable of manifesting his or her heart's desires. In *The Power of Awareness,* Neville emphatically explains that "To be transformed, the whole basis of your thoughts must change. But your thoughts cannot change unless you have *new ideas,* for you think from your ideas."[3] How do you find the way to ideas that will help you change your thoughts? Start by saying and writing an affirmation that appeals to you. Create your unique heartfelt affirmation, such as: *I have a burning desire— an inner flame that will not be extinguished by outer forces—to know and live from higher regions, to be transformed so that my new concept of myself will no longer include any limitations. I am willing to challenge and change any thoughts that impede my having a higher vision of myself.*

Before closing this introductory chapter, it will be helpful to explore your beliefs about the nature of those things we call thoughts, and how to change them.

Do You Really Think?

No one has ever been able to say from whence a thought comes, or what that thought is made up of. It's generally accepted that we think up things and we make up all of our own thoughts. To be perfectly honest, for a large portion of my life, I held these same views on thoughts originating with each individual. But at this juncture I tend to see the entire process as more of an act of observation, contemplation, and choice. I enjoy noticing that I have a continuous stream of thoughts that come from . . . who knows where? They have no boundaries or forms to examine, and apparently are unlimited in number and permutation! I think of the stock market ticker that runs along the bottom of a screen, with each stock price representing a simple thought.

You are capable of thinking many opposing thoughts in just a few moments, jumping helter-skelter from one idea to another—exhilaration, frustration, fear, ecstasy, worry, and so forth. Unguided and unguarded, you serve up an endless array of thoughts continuously from waking to falling asleep. Even while sound asleep, your mind continues observing, grabbing, and contemplating these omnipresent thoughts. There's very little respite from this mental thought-producing process throughout your entire lifetime. If you really believe that you are the creator of all of your thoughts and control the entire process, then simply stop. That's right, just try to stop thinking. You may be able to slow the stream of thoughts down considerably, but to simply stop thinking all day and stay in a thoughtless state is quite impossible.

I'm suggesting you open your thought processes to a new idea that will help you as you begin changing your concept of yourself. You can think of yourself as a Divine limitless being rather than a person who doesn't have choice when it comes to your thoughts. Think of yourself as an observer, contemplating and selecting thoughts that you choose from that never-ending stream of thoughts on your inner screen, 24/7/365. Watch thoughts stream by from wherever they originate, and observe them rapidly transitioning and combining and appearing and disappearing. Snatch a thought from the running ribbon of thoughts and contemplate it. As you toss it around, notice how you feel—sad, depressed, happy, frightened, and so on. Every thought going by has an imprint on your concept of yourself. First be the observer, and then the contemplator. Now become the choice maker who can consciously decide to put that thought back into the running stream and pick a different one, a thought that perhaps allows you to feel better.

I am okay, I look fine, I will lose a few pounds, I am loved, I am Divine . . . these and millions more like them are thoughts that you can opt for rather than the ones you've become accustomed to choosing in the past. This is how you begin a new process to change your concept of yourself. You accept as irrevocable that it is not you setting the stream of thoughts into motion, and that stopping thinking isn't possible at this stage of your evolution. At this stage the essence of your being is to observe, contemplate, and then choose. This can all be done in a fraction of a nanosecond. The thoughts will keep appearing on your mental TV screen just like the stock quotations. But you'll now be choosing the ones you want to focus on, gather, retain, or let go.

I'm encouraging you to initiate a habit of choosing thoughts and ideas that support feeling good and powerful, and that elevate you to a higher level of consciousness where your self-concept welcomes your higher self.

I love Uell S. Andersen's description of this process in his book *Three Magic Words*. I leave you to contemplate it as you prepare to befriend that indwelling self that is desperately wishing to be fulfilled at the extraordinary level, rather than at the ordinary where you have lived for far too long:

> We have assured the indwelling Self that it can be anything it accepts and has faith in, and we are now about to develop in it the habit of choosing only those thoughts and ideas that will constructively add good unto it. We are teaching ourselves to accept only good. . . . We are deliberately compelling ourselves to accept all love, all kindness, all hope, all joy, all expansion, all abundance, all health, all vigor. We are deliberately compelling ourselves to reject all suffering, all sorrow, all depression,

all morbidness, all inferiority, all aches and pains. We are saying nothing is true but the great and the good and the beautiful, only these will we add unto ourselves.

This is your new way of choosing thoughts that will introduce you to what I am calling your highest self—keeping uppermost in mind that if you want to accomplish something (anything), you must first expect it of yourself.

Three Suggestions

— Redefine your self-concept by challenging everything that you've held to be true about yourself up until now. Be open to examining everything you've previously thought limited you in any way. Affirm: *I place no limits and no restrictions on all that I intend to accomplish and become from here on in.*

— Allow yourself to become aware of the nonphysical reality that you are a part of. Reach out to the angels or occupants of this higher invisible plane. Know that you can access guidance from those who've lived here before. Spend time in meditation accessing the feelings of a plane of higher consciousness.

— Whenever you're experiencing discomfort or sadness, rather than trying to change the thought behind your emotional state, instead just put it back onto the never-ending conveyor belt of thoughts, and then select a different thought. Keep doing this until you've selected a thought that allows you to feel good, and you're no longer condemning yourself for creating unhappy thoughts.

YOUR HIGHER SELF

*"From the beginning I had a sense of destiny, as though my life
was assigned to me by fate and had to be fulfilled. This gave me
an inner security, and, though I could never prove it to myself, it
proved itself to me. I did not have the certainty, <u>it</u> had me."*

— CARL JUNG

For the past 18 months or so I've been deeply involved in the
study of what is known as *initiatic science,* the principal goal of
which is to help the initiate/student (meaning you and me) know
and trust in the higher self. These ancient teachings repeatedly
explain that emphasizing only the needs of our physical self, and
ignoring the needs of the higher self, results in the soul and spirit
suffocating and dying of hunger and thirst. The initiates of old
insisted on the importance of the knowledge of the higher self because this awareness opens up tremendous possibilities for growth,
progress, and, yes—the ability to have one's wishes fulfilled.

Perhaps it is difficult to imagine yourself so divided as to produce both a higher and a lower self. Very likely this idea of a self
within yourself, which is higher than what you think of as your
real self, is foreign to your way of thinking. I have long referred to
this lower self or false self as the ego—a part of you that believes

you're defined by what you achieve, own, or win. It's a belief that whatever status you've accumulated is proof that you're a separate being possessing particular strengths or limitations. It probably isn't a surprise that I suggest there are different beliefs that can and will put you on the path of happiness, success, and health that you desire.

This idea of having a higher self that transcends the *self* descriptor derived from almost universal identification with the ego may be difficult to internalize. If you've read the first chapter of this book, then you know that it's necessary that you *make the choice* to change what you believe is true. Remind yourself that your current concept of who you are has landed you right here, reading a book on how to become a more powerful person.

Are you willing to internalize radical new ideas that require a shift in your concept of yourself? Are you receptive to the idea of having a higher self that isn't defined by ego concerns? Are you able to entertain the idea of an unlimited higher self that is within you? Can you imagine that you can eschew ego's limiting demands that are keeping you stuck at an ordinary level of consciousness? In other words, can you approach the question of *Who am I?* with complete unknowing? Conceiving the idea of a higher self begins with this personal inner query. So let's first examine this question of who you are.

Who Am I?

Consider how many bodies you've occupied since birth. Who is the I that continues to leave one body behind and then enter another? You know for certain that you—the person that you call I, the one attempting to figure out who you are—started out in a little baby body weighing somewhere between five and ten pounds. The I that is you fully entered and occupied that little baby body. Gradually you began to discard that baby body and move into a small toddler body that crawled, then walked, then ran, and took on an entirely new appearance. Your two-year-old self would find it difficult to recognize the baby body that you'd now completely abandoned. You lived in this toddler body for a while and then discarded it, too, including every cell that was in your body at birth. The subsequent body you entered was a pre-pubescent body that bore a similarity to your toddler body but was completely different.

The I in the question still hasn't been discovered, but it's become absolutely clear that you are obviously not your body. Why? Because the I has remained, though it continuously sheds the body that it occupies. This strange phenomenon of you being an I that continuously enters, discards, and reenters a new body has proceeded right up until this very moment.

I am currently in a 70-year-old body that's nothing like the body I occupied 50 years ago. I remember well what that 20-year-old body I occupied looked like, what it could do, and what it knew and didn't know, but I can't find it anywhere—it's simply an illusion. It is gone from this physical world, as is every body that both you and I have occupied in our lifetime. The I that I use to describe myself is not so obsessed that he insists upon staying only in one body. In fact, that I that is me finally recognizes the ancient spiritual truth spoken by Divine masters since antiquity: *None of us are really doing anything, rather we (our bodies) are merely being done.*

What is your body being done by? An invisible organizing intelligence that takes the cells of your body, changes them into new cells, and discards the old cells. The I that you think you are observes the entire process—for the most part, helplessly. The physical body that you think of as you is rearranged in a pattern designed by a formless intelligence independent of your opinions. This I that you use to describe yourself isn't the physical form that you occupy and take with you everywhere. Quantum physics states that the body you're occupying, which is reading this paragraph right now, is completely different from the body you were in when you read the previous paragraph. Such is the nature of the physical world in which we all live.

The ancient philosopher Heraclitus put it this way several thousand years ago, and it is true today: "All things are in motion and nothing is at rest. . . . You cannot go into the same [river] twice." A river is a constantly changing phenomenon, as is a tree, a mountain, a goat, a human, and the physical universe including Earth. That which defines a thing, therefore, is not physical in nature; it is metaphysical. When asked "What is real?" an ancient spiritual avatar responded without hesitation, "That is real which never changes." And since your body is in a continuous state of change, it is not real.

If you try to find that toddler body you once occupied, you realize that it is not real, since it no longer exists. Even while you were in it years ago, you couldn't call it real, because the moment you pinpointed and defined it as real, it would be something else, something new. What you're calling real would already have disappeared. Still, you know with all of this change taking place that there is a changeless component to who you are. The I in that toddler body hasn't changed, it is in the body that you currently occupy. The I is your higher self, changeless and real. This higher self is who you are. When you make this discovery and consciously befriend the I you are, nothing is impossible.

In Chapter One I explained the necessity of creating a new concept of yourself: as an infinite spiritual being having a temporary, human experience. As you read on, keep in mind that *if it is changing, it is not real.* The I in the question *Who am I?* isn't anything that involves the physical you, since that continuously changes and disappears. Therefore, to answer the question *Who am I?* with any reference to your body and its various talents, accomplishments, accumulations, or physical prowess is to *define yourself as unreal.* Who you are, then, must be *changeless,* and therefore *birthless* as well as *deathless.* Who you are is a formless energy—a *spirit,* if you will—with the capacity to be unchanged, and at the same time occupy an infinity of bodies.

Think about this—it is truly a bewildering phenomenon. You are changeless and therefore *real.* What you've believed were facts explaining who you are, are simply illusions—or what metaphysicians call *unreal.* You were convinced by some well-intentioned relatives, teachers, and cultural influences that you were really this ego of yours, when in fact everything that the ego uses to define you is disappearing as fast as you can assess it. Your possessions, achievements, reputations, trophies, bank accounts—even your family members, including your children—are all aspects of a world that is changing, dissolving to nothingness . . . all unreal.

Here is how a brilliant scribe described this phenomenon poetically:

> *This quiet Dust was Gentlemen and Ladies*
> *And Lads and Girls;*
> *Was laughter and ability and sighing,*
> *And frocks and curls.*
> *This passive place a summer's nimble mansion,*
> *Where Bloom and Bees*
> *Fulfilled their Oriental Circuit,*
> *Then ceased like these.*

In this poem, Emily Dickinson reminds you with her dazzling honesty that all ceases and turns to dust—everything you may have believed was the real you, including the body and all of its accomplishments, and even its laughing and sighing. But the real I that is you can smile at all of those lower-self, ego-identified proceedings. Your higher self exists beyond that lower, false self. It is in fact higher than all of your earthbound identities.

You have a self that can look down from a more exalted position upon that lower, ego-dominated self. So begin to know yourself as something far greater than the ever-changing, ever-dying aspects that have dominated your picture of who you are. *Who am I?* is then answered with, *I am an infinite being who originated not from my parents, but from a Source that is itself birthless, deathless, and changeless.*

Your Connection to Source

We have all been created from the same Source, and it is my conclusion that we must be like what we came from. It matters not what we call this Source. *The Tao that can be named, is not the eternal Tao* is the message in the opening lines of the Tao Te Ching. Call it Tao, call it God, call it Jehovah, call it Divine mind—it matters not. You are merely interested in recognizing that you originated from the Source of all life in a form you know as your constantly changing physical body, which obviously contains the creative energy that you came from.

Read these words, recorded during a 1967 lecture given by an initiatic science master, Omraam Mikhaël Aïvanhov:

> The creator has planted within every creature a fragment of himself, a spark, a spirit of the same nature as himself and, thanks to this spirit, every creature can become a creator. And this means that, instead of always waiting for their needs to be satisfied by some external source, human beings can work inwardly by means of their thought, their will, and their spirit to obtain the nourishing healing elements they need. This is why the teaching I bring you is of the spirit, of the creator and not of matter . . .

I love this quote because it speaks to a part of you that has been largely ignored throughout all of your educational pursuits and accomplishments. The key words here are "a fragment of himself, a spark" that lies within you, but has largely been left unexamined. This is a great image for you to begin to understand the greatness of your higher self. There is a spark of God within you that is the invisibleness I've been alluding to. It is that which you cannot grasp with the senses—it beats your heart, grows your hair, and keeps your lungs breathing in and breathing out. You've become accustomed to taking it for granted while putting the major focus of your life on the physical (unreal) you.

My objective in this chapter and the next is to inspire you to recognize that a spark—a tiny fragment of the creative source of the universe—is located within you, and to help you increase the power of that spark so it becomes the primary force in your everyday life. Review the first chapter and affirm your willingness to change your concept of yourself to help you recognize and increase that spark. Then dedicate yourself to exploring this higher self I'm writing about.

Your higher self is that spark, but a spark is an infinitesimal portion of your physical being. If you weigh 150 pounds, that spark weighs maybe 1/100th of an ounce. This is only a symbolic image (because the "spark" is unchanging), but I'm encouraging you to conceptualize that spark of God inside of you. Imagine it growing to double its size, then a tenfold spark, then maybe a shred, then a segment, then a chunk, then a lump, then a piece or a section . . . and just perceive that spark of God as the real you becoming visible through your loving and inviting attentiveness, until you feel the sacred presence of your higher self as the guiding light of your life.

Ultimately, as I'll discuss later, it will overtake the you that's been dominated by ego and your sensory apparatus. That former speck of a spark will be the foundation of your life. You might conceptualize this former spark as a sacred light inside of your head that is the same size as your brain. Now you have a big piece of God to assist you in attaining a status wherein the fulfillment of your wishes becomes a no-brainer, or perhaps you'd call it a new-brainer. This new brain is comprised exclusively of infinite God energy.

Your Higher Self at Work Every Day

I want you to seriously contemplate another observation made by the initiatic spiritual master Omraam Mikhaël Aïvanhov, in a lecture given in January 1971: "Our higher self is perfect, omniscient and almighty, a fragment of God Himself, a pure, transparent, luminous quintessence."

This will very likely be a challenge for you as you consider a new concept of yourself by accepting some truths that you have been raised to believe are falsehoods. Yet I ask you to study this ancient spiritual teaching, which is designed to familiarize you with a radical idea about the powers you possess just by the fact that you are a living, breathing human being. If you are committed to accessing your higher consciousness, then you must be willing to do what is required in order to integrate what this great initiatic teacher is offering.

In order to accomplish becoming an almighty being, your higher self (God) must be enlarged from a spark to a more meaningful portion of your essence. Since you are a piece of God and therefore have that within you, you needn't doubt your own divinity. As Jesus reminds you, "Is it not written in your law, 'I said, "You are gods"'?" (John 10:34). As a growing spark of God, you must be willing to say, "That portion of myself that has not edged God out (ego) must be perfect; it is all-knowing and it is almighty. There is nothing that this higher self that I am cannot accomplish."

Once again, let's look at something Jesus told us: "With God all things are possible" (Matthew 19:26). *All things are possible* leaves nothing out. As my teachers in the initiatic sciences frequently reminded me, this higher self—that portion of God that is us—only begins to notice us and give us the attention we crave when we enlarge it from a tiny spark and invite the energy into our life.

Your awareness that God isn't something external to you but rather a *portion* of yourself is truly a giant step in your spiritual evolution. You can tell yourself with genuine knowing, *I am perfect.* (All forms of *I am* have tremendous significance, as you will learn when you delve into the next chapter on your *highest* self.) In this chapter you are discovering your *higher* self. God no longer resides outside of you, and no longer plays favorites. In short, you've revised humankind's image of a god created in its own egoistic idea of itself.

A god who knows how to heal yet withholds healing from some and offers it to others who are presumed to have paid some kind of dues? A god who is angry? A god who gives humans the pleasure of sexuality but promises to burn in hell those who don't follow rules devised by other humans? A god who gives us eyes and remains invisible, but threatens damnation for those who don't believe in him? A god who demands to be paid for services, with fancy temples and gold-lined costumes for his highest representatives? This is a god of the ego.

Your higher self is a piece of an all-loving, all-embracing creative Source. All you need do is accept that this is not something external to yourself. It resides within you (the kingdom of heaven is within)—in fact, it *is* you—and all you need do is begin to align yourself with this Divine essence, begin to act like it acts and think like it thinks, and you will begin the process of manifesting just as it does. This is the true essence of living a life in which your wishes are fulfilled. Give your Divine nature a chance. (The second part of this book provides a step-by-step plan for allowing your higher self to take over the process of fulfilling your desires.)

In these opening chapters, I hope to jar you into an awareness of how powerful a being you really are when you get past so much of the nonsensical conditioning that has dominated your enculturation. Toss out any self-limiting ideas about your Divine nature and what it is capable of achieving. Befriend that spark, consult it frequently, nurture it, pay close attention to it, believe in it, and practice describing yourself first as a spiritual being—one who lives as frequently as possible from this all-loving, all-giving, all-joyful place called your higher self. Your higher self is just what it says: higher than your false self, higher than your material physical self. It is the part of you that is aligned with your very Source of being.

In the next chapter, you have the opportunity to consider an even more unlikely assertion in light of all that you've been exposed to since childhood. Not only do you have a lower ego-based false self, as well as a spiritually based higher self that is a piece of God, but you have a *highest self.* A self that you have been trained to believe is not something that you should ever claim. Your highest self awaits you in Chapter Three.

Three Suggestions

— Set aside multiple times during your day to stop and ask yourself this key question: *Right now in what I am about to say or do, do my desires stem from my lower or my higher self?* The ego is all about self-serving, ownership, winning, judging, and so on. The higher self is about serving, loving, and being in a nonjudgmental state of peace. Ask yourself this question, and create the opportunity to align yourself more fully with God. You then have access to the same powers of manifestation as your Source of being. This question, when honestly explored, helps you align with the power to fulfill your wishes and desires. You don't need to abolish your ego animal nature. You do need to keep it tamed so it isn't allowed to overshadow or destroy your spirit. Give your Divine nature a chance by asking yourself this question.

— Spend some of your quiet meditation time visualizing a tiny spark of awareness glowing within your being. Practice seeing this God-portion of yourself expanding its glow within your mind. See it growing into a personally satisfying size. Continue this expansion exercise sensing the spark/glow as your God essence. You will begin acting from this inner God-realized image.

— Use these affirmations frequently: *I am all-knowing, I am all-powerful, I am unlimited.* This helps you banish doubt and refer to this portion of yourself that lives in a spiritual world of no restrictions. Simply affirm to yourself without explaining to others or demonstrating pride in what you're doing. You are ridding yourself of ego-dominated mental messages that continue to want to convince you that you are primarily your body and its five senses.

YOUR HIGHEST SELF

*"Let this mind be in you which was also
in Christ Jesus, who, being in the form of God,
did not consider it robbery to be equal with God."*

— PHILIPPIANS 2:5-6

In the previous chapter you explored the idea that there's a spark of God within you, which you can choose to expand into a consciously larger component of your daily life. This spark is your spiritual essence—your higher self. As your awareness increases that you are a God-realized being, you will welcome it as the central focus of your life.

The concept of your *higher self* will gradually evolve into your *highest self,* which is truly omniscient, almighty, and capable of producing miracles. Here you will see a new reality—a majestic idea of yourself that previously seemed inconceivable. Your highest self is described in the pronouncement in the display quote at the beginning of this chapter, written by Saint Paul in his letters to the Philippians in the New Testament. You move from being a spark or a fragment of God to being able to assert that *I am God* and not feel as if you're committing blasphemy or a cardinal sin by such a declaration. Here, the idea that you are equal with God was promoted by Christ Jesus, and you are encouraged by him to "Let this mind be in you . . ."

This isn't the God created by humans—the ego-driven deity who plays favorites, requires ostentatious places of worship, has temper tantrums, demands reparations, and is filled with rage, punishing those who do not do his bidding. Not even close! I am speaking here of the creative Source of all being, a God Who is responsible for creating the miraculous movement from nonbeing to being, a God Who is formless—Who does nothing yet leaves nothing undone—a God Who is everywhere. This is a Divine invisible presence that's within you. This idea is at the basis of all great spiritual teaching throughout all time.

Much of organized religious teaching proclaims that *God is an all-powerful being outside of you.* That idea has been thrown at you since you were old enough to process this absurd notion. God, you were told, watches you and punishes you if you misbehave, but listens to your prayers and helps you resolve your conflicts if you do the right thing and please Him.

Perhaps it is a radical idea for you to declare, "I am God" and "God is love," or believe that "He who abides in love abides in God, and God in him" (1 John 4:16) is who you are. When you are this God, this essence of pure love, it is all you have to give away, and when you realign yourself in this vein (once again quoting Jesus the Christ), "With men this is impossible, but with God all things are possible." Now, *all things are possible* leaves out nothing, including your ability to fulfill any and all wishes that are aligned with God.

You may find it difficult at first to be able to assert to yourself that *I am God.* But when you put it into the context of God as love (and pure love allows you to be almighty, all-knowing, and God-realized), you will, I assure you, begin to regain the omnipotence that is your essence from the moment of your transition from nonbeing (spirit) to being (human). I emphasize these teachings of Jesus to show that the declaration of *I am God* is not only *not* in opposition to the teachings of Christianity or other spiritual practices, but is fully aligned with these earlier teachings. The reason it may seem blasphemous to say that *I am God* is because we've adopted the God of the ego, created by humans from ego-based ideas of a God that imitates our most unholy human attributes.

I've been studying two great spiritual teachers in depth for several years as I've prepared to write this book. One of them is Uell S. Andersen, and the book of his that I read, studied, meditated upon, and am now living and teaching is titled *Three Magic Words*. The book is 323 pages long, and it was not until the last chapter—after many specific meditations and exercises; after many enlightening words on consciousness, intuition, faith, love, success, immortality, and more; and after investing time and energy in what is being taught by the author—that I discovered what the three magic words actually are.

Here is the beginning of the final chapter, titled "The Key":

> This is the ineffable secret, the ultimate illumination, the key to peace and power: *You are God.* If you will accept this towering truth, dare to stand atop this magnificent pinnacle, universal consciousness will be revealed to you from within. God is there. It is He who peers from behind your eyes, who is your own consciousness, who is your very Self. You are not just a part of God; you are *altogether* God, and God is *altogether you.*

This is your highest self. It's indeed a towering assumption—but one, if used in context and alignment with the creative Source of all, that is the key to mastering the ability to live a life of your wishes being fulfilled. After all, with God as you, and you as God, all things are possible. This is not an assertion limited to Western teachings or the Christian faith. In the Vedanta, the ancient, pre-Christian teachings, we are reminded that we are not a part of, but identical with, that absolute spirit of the world.

Before we go any further, I want to share with you some words from my other great spiritual teacher, Neville, regarding this notion of you and me actually being God.

Neville's book *The Power of Awareness* contains 27 brief chapters—it's a book you could easily read in a couple of hours. Yet much like the Tao Te Ching, though it can be read in a brief amount of time, it could also be studied endlessly and you'd repeatedly discover deeper meaning. (As I mentioned earlier, I devoted a year to studying, meditating on, practicing, and ultimately writing essays on how to apply the wisdom of that tiny little book of 81 verses. The result was published as a compendium titled *Change Your Thoughts—Change Your Life: Living the Wisdom of the Tao*.) Neville's brief book had the same kind of magnetic allure for me as did the Tao. It was in my seventh complete reading of Neville's book, and after listening to some of his recorded lectures, that I decided to write this book in an effort to make his stupendous insights more readily available and applicable to those of us now occupying this planet as temporary residents.

I've taken extensive notes on Neville's teaching and literally put them to work in my own life. I have lectured throughout the world on the idea of having our wishes fulfilled via the avenue of assuming the power of God that is not only our birthright, but our very essence. Neville's words remind me to seek my highest self, and whenever I make the decision to live from this awareness, I am immediately at peace, and watch as Divine consciousness seems to align with me in creating the fulfillment of all that I ask for.

As I finished the first 26 chapters in my seventh reading of Neville, I heard once again the same holy refrain that U. S. Andersen offered in his conclusion of *Three Magic Words*. Neville begins his final chapter, titled "Reverence," with these words:

> In all creation, in all eternity, in all the realms of your infinite being the most wonderful fact is that which is stressed in the first chapter of this book. *You are God.* You are the "I am that I am." You are consciousness. You are the creator. This is the mystery, this is the great secret known by the seers, prophets, and mystics throughout the ages. This is the truth that you can never know *intellectually.* . . . The important thing is that *it is within you, it is you, it is your world.*[4]

This is a monumental awareness—a knowing that you can only feel. It manifests as a feeling of love that is ineffable, and incapable of being known intellectually. Neville's conclusion explains this perfectly:

> The knowledge that your creator is the very self of yourself and never would have made you had he not *loved you* must fill your heart with devotion, yes, with adoration. . . . It is when your feeling of reverence is most intense that you are closest to God, and *when you are closest to God, your life is richest.*[5]

I conclude that the closest you can be to God is through recognizing what this entire chapter is about—you can't be any closer to God than to *be* God. When you realize this preeminent assertion, you regain the power of your Source because you no longer live as if you were estranged from your Source. You see that God manifests in a countless array of forms, and yes, you are one of those sublime forms.

In Neville's conclusion that you are God, he uses the phrase, "You are the 'I am that I am.'" These five words are an absolutely crucial component of the essence of this book. They will be extremely helpful in getting you over the hurdle of truly knowing that you are God. Why? Because you've most likely been conditioned to believe that such an assertion is blasphemous and likely to incur God's wrath by daring to question His supremacy.

A Journey into the I Am That I Am

As has always happened with my writing, there seem to be unseen forces that direct me as I move forward on my own spiritual path, fulfilling a dharma that Carl Jung also expressed about his life's work. Like him, I've often felt that "sense of destiny, as though my life was assigned to me by fate and had to be fulfilled." Jung also said that this gave him an "inner security," which I identify with as well. And though he couldn't prove it, he said that "it proved itself to me. I did not have the certainty, it had me."

Throughout my entire professional career, when I've felt tugged toward a newer and a higher spiritual place, I too have felt guided. It's as if angels send me information related to what I will be writing and experiencing—long before the actual writing/ speaking. Strangers send me a variety of media to listen to or to read that awakens something within me. Repeated references in conversation or reviews about movies will ignite an inner spark of inquisitiveness, which leads to what I didn't know I needed for my next step up on the ladder to enlightened living.

This was true as I was preparing myself (or possibly being prepared) for examining this idea of spiritual wish fulfillment. The work of Neville kept knocking at my door in a myriad of ways, as did initiatic science and U. S. Andersen's *Three Magic Words*. But the teachings that I'd need to study, experience, and ultimately know had to penetrate my consciousness. How was my council of angelic immortals going to get this information to me, this ancient teaching that I had been almost totally removed from for my entire life? As I've said many times, when the student is ready, the teachers will appear.

I feel that I was being made ready, and the teachers and teachings were showing up in just the right way to prod me toward the fulfillment of my own dharma, and perhaps yours, too—since you are now reading these words and are therefore connected to all that I am being taught as well. Obviously, we are all in this thing together. Your being in possession of this book and studying the messages herein may be just as mysterious to you as how the teachings came to me.

I had been away from my writing space on Maui for several months, speaking and spending time with my family. When I returned, I received a call from my yoga teacher telling me that someone had dropped off a package at the studio for me. When I picked it up it was like a gift from King Midas—wrapped in gold paper with a beautiful ribbon tied in a bow. I brought it home and set the gift next to my eating space and looked at it every day for three weeks, each time thinking it was just one more package to open amongst the mountain of mail that had accumulated over the previous months in my absence. But there was something unique about this package, so I just left it there through all of my meals, telling myself, *I'll open it later,* yet feeling strangely drawn to it at the same time.

One evening I finally decided to open it, and I must say I had a rush of excitement that I couldn't understand at the time. As I undid the bow, I discovered a note attached to the box, written to me by a Ms. Carol Ann Jacobs, whom I did not know, nor had I even met. She had heard through the grapevine that I practiced yoga at the Lahaina studio and simply left it there to be given to me when I returned. The note said:

> *This gift of gold is a pearl of the highest wisdom on the planet, handed down through the ethers from the Octave of Light. If taken up, used, and made as a living flame within oneself—it will lead them into their ascension at the close of this embodiment.*
>
> ♥ *With sincere love and gratitude for all the raising of the vibration you have done for the earth, and for all the "beings of the elements."*
>
> *Lovingly,*
> *Carol Ann Jacobs*

As I unwrapped the gold paper, I saw that the box contained a small book, which I immediately decided (I thought) that I couldn't possibly read, since I had at least 25 books from all over the world with requests for me to read, endorse, or write a Fore-word. Because of the volume of such material that perpetually shows up at my doorstep, I always have a large number of books that I donate to charities. I left the book on the table and said to myself, *I'll put this with the others destined to be donated to a worthy cause. I simply can't get to it.*

But this little package seemed to have an energy all of its own. I'd glance at it, peruse it a bit, and then set it down, vowing to put it on the pile of materials that I would never get to. Yet it remained next to me for several weeks. One day while I was holding it, I felt a shaft of energy course through me. I had goose bumps all over my body. And thus began a new chapter in my life. I decided right there and then that I would read the entire 362 pages. The contents of this book led me to further inquiry, which culminated in *my?* (probably not mine) decision to put these gold nuggets of spiritual truth into my speeches and writing—and, most important, my life. The book is Volume Three in the Saint Germain Series, titled *The "I AM" Discourses.*

In my daily reading of the material, I began to see clearly the message of you and I and everyone else being God. The 33 discourses in this volume were channeled directly from the ascended master Saint Germain and others, including Jesus Christ, between October 3, 1932, and January 1, 1935—when they were published as *The "I AM" Discourses.*

Guy Ballard was the man present for these dictations, and he published them under his pseudonym Godfre Ray King. He writes:

> The thirty-three Discourses contained in this book were dictated over a visible Light and Sound Ray in our home during 1932 by the Ascended Master Saint Germain and those other Ascended Masters directly concerned with this Activity. The sound of His Voice was physically audible to everyone in the room. . . . Never before, except in the Retreats of the Great White Brotherhood, has such intensified, transcendent Instruction concerning the "I AM" been given to individuals.[6]

I am simply presenting this to you as what is written in the Foreword of the book. It is of no concern to me to delve into the veracity or authenticity of channeled material—to me, everything is channeled from God. I don't know where these words I'm writing come from—I certainly don't own them, and I feel that they come fast and furious when I stay in spirit or inspired. What I *am* concerned with is the magnificence of these messages and my awareness that our world could be a world of love, peace, and joy; and we have the power to access unlimited fulfillment of wishes that are aligned with our source of being. And that is why I present the essence of the "I AM" teachings and encourage you to dig deeply into their content. The essence is quite simply that *I am* is the full activity of God, and that each and every one of us can realign ourselves so that our *I ams* reflect the God that we are, rather than the ego that most of us have become.

Here is one more very important observation from the First Discourse offered by Saint Germain:

> The first expression of every individual, everywhere in the Universe, either in spoken word, silent thought or feeling is "I AM," recognizing Its Own Conquering Divinity.
>
> The student, endeavoring to understand and apply these mighty, yet simple Laws, must stand guard more strictly over his thought and expression—in word or otherwise; for every time you say "I AM not," "I cannot," "I have not," you are, whether knowingly or unknowingly, throttling that "Great Presence" within you.[7]

This speaks so directly to me and the message I wish to convey. Every time you think of the expression *I Am,* you initiate God in action. Why not continually remind yourself that *I live, move, and have my being as God, the I am that I am?*

I'm going to detour here for a few paragraphs to bring you back to a transmission that is recorded in a book that you're probably familiar with, which is the Holy Bible—both the Torah (the first five books of the Old Testament) and the New Testament. If you've been raised Christian or Jewish, you will see that these tidings of spiritual truth I'm delivering here are dramatically harmonized with your core teachings. These five words—*I am that I am*—contain a message that has been encoded in your soul. According to ancient spiritual teachings dating back 1,300 years before the birth of Christ, the words *I am* align you with the Divine, and at the same time remind you that you are the Divine, possessing the same power to create as God.

God Speaks as I Am

The infant Moses, you may recall, was put in a basket and left in the reeds by the Nile River because he was the son of an Israelite slave. The pharaoh had ordered every male child born to Israelite slaves to be drowned in the river. However, as luck or Divine intervention would have it, the pharaoh's daughter discovered the floating infant and rescued him to be raised as a prince among his despotic enemies.

As a young man, Moses witnesses an Egyptian soldier abusing an Israelite slave and responds by killing the soldier and hiding the body. But his adoptive grandfather the pharaoh discovers his misdeed and orders him put to death. Moses escapes to the land of Midian and finds refuge with Jethro, a local priest, whose daughter Zipporah he marries. Moses lives primarily as a shepherd and husband for some 40 years.

Now here is a man born to an Israelite slave, who was supposed to be killed at birth by order of the pharaoh but was saved by the pharaoh's daughter and raised as her son, and is now a shepherd. He's out tending his flock when he encounters a burning bush, which continues to burn without consuming the bush itself. Moses, then, the ancient scriptures tell us, hears God speaking:

> And the Angel of the Lord appeared to him in a flame of fire from the midst of a bush. So he looked, and behold, the bush was burning with fire, but the bush was not consumed. . . . God called to him from the midst of the bush and said, "Moses, Moses!" And he said, "Here I am." Then He said, "Do not draw near this place. Take your sandals off your feet, for the place where you stand is holy ground." Moreover, He said, "I am the God of your father—the God of Abraham, the God of Isaac, and the God of Jacob" (Exodus 3:2–6).

The story continues in the book of Exodus, and God was said to have told Moses that he was to go to the pharaoh and free the children of Israel, saying, "Come now, therefore, and I will send you to Pharaoh that you may bring My people, the children of Israel, out of Egypt" (Exodus 3:10).

Then Moses questions how he could do such an enormous task all by himself, and God replies, "I will certainly be with you" (Exodus 3:12). Moses follows up by inquiring, "Indeed, when I come to the children of Israel and say to them, 'The God of your fathers has sent me to you,' and they say to me, 'What is His name?' what shall I say to them?" (Exodus 3:13). "And God said to Moses, 'I AM THAT I AM.' And He said, Thus you shall say to the children of Israel, "I AM has sent me to you." . . . This is My name forever, and this is My memorial to all generations'" (Exodus 3:14–15).

This is also a memorial to you and me in this generation. The name of God, which is you and me, is *I am*. This is the fundamental teaching of *The "I AM" Discourses* and becoming acquainted with your highest self.

Still having trouble seeing yourself as God? Try this: Imagine God as the ocean. If you take a bucket of water out of the ocean, is the water in the bucket the ocean? Yes, indeed, it is altogether ocean—and the ocean, even though it is larger, is still altogether the whole of the ocean in the bucket. Now think of yourself as a bucket of God. Altogether God; and God is altogether you. It is only when you stay separated from the ocean that the water dries up. This is your task in grasping your highest self—staying aligned and not separated from your Source, and remembering what God says in Psalms 46:10: "Be still, and know that I am God."

In *The Moses Code,* author James Twyman makes a powerful case for getting to this truth—in fact, the subtitle is, "The Most Powerful Manifestation Tool in the History of the World." (I also encourage you to read James's fascinating book for a much fuller treatment of the power of the words that God reputedly spoke to Moses in response to his question regarding His name.)

The Torah is presumed to have been written some 1,300 years before the birth of Christ. The holy place where God first manifests and tells Moses to remove his shoes is where Moses discovers who he truly is by his very first words to God: "Here I am."

I say this to you with absolute certainty—the *I am* that has been with you in all the physical forms you've occupied since your birth is God. The two words *I am* are God's name. How do you use these words? You strive to *know*—just like God taught when He said, "Be still, and know that I am God"—that with the use of God's name, you release all doubt about being able to manifest

59

your desires, and you live from the exalted pinnacle of your highest self.

Just to reinforce this idea that you are indeed the I am that I am, or God, consider moving forward to the time when Jesus the man was on Earth. His words let you know that this idea of declaring yourself as *I Am God* is not some New Age interpretation, and in no way is offensive to Christianity. You are not guilty of blasphemy by allowing this belief to be alive within you. If you're experiencing pangs of guilt, reread the display quote at the beginning of this chapter, which was written by Saint Paul. Yes, you are equal with God. It's okay!

Jesus Speaks As I Am

In the book of John, when Jesus is asked if he has *seen* Abraham, he responds with these words: "Most assuredly, I say to you, before Abraham was, I AM" (John 8:58). Here Jesus indicates that God, the creative Source of the universe, defined as love, is called I Am. Throughout the New Testament, many of the most significant messages offered to all of us begin with the name of God— a name that you too have come to use. All too frequently, though, you use it to define yourself as a part of, or distant from, your Source: *I am weak, I am sick, I am poor, I am sad,* and so on.

By using the words *I am,* Jesus tells us that he is one with God. He doesn't just say the name, he claims it as himself, and, as you will soon see, asks you to do the same. Here is James Twyman in *The Moses Code:* "When Jesus came along and basically said, 'I AM God,' they responded in the harshest manner. And yet, this is the essence of the Moses Code—the realization that we're all one with God, and once realized, to act with the power and passion of God in the world. When Jesus did this, miracles followed him everywhere he went."

And I say to you emphatically that by internalizing this message and knowing it, you too will have miracles occurring in your life.

60

Here are some of those powerful messages from the teachings of Jesus, in which he invokes the name of God as a prefix to his admonitions to all of us.

"I am the door. If anyone enters by Me, he will be saved" (John 10:9).

"I am the good shepherd" (John 10:11).

"I am the bread of life. He who comes to Me shall never hunger, and he who believes in me shall never thirst" (John 6:35).

"I am the light of the world. He who follows Me shall not walk in darkness, but have the light of life" (John 8:12).

"I am the way, the truth, and the life. No one comes to the Father except through Me" (John 14:6).

"I am the true vine, and My Father is the vinedresser" (John 15:1).

"I am the vine, you are the branches. He who abides in Me, and I in him, bears much fruit; for without Me you can do nothing" (John 15:5).

"I am the Alpha and the Omega, the Beginning and the End" (Rev 1:8).

And perhaps the most significant I am statement offered by Jesus:

"I am the resurrection and the life. He who believes in Me, though he may die, he shall live" (John 11:25).

Note that Jesus did not say "I am the crucifixion." He said, "I am the resurrection," meaning God is the resurrection, the being of light that is eternal and resides in all of us.

When my youngest daughter, Saje, was a second grader in a private religious school, she told her mother and me that she hated going into the chapel and seeing a dead body impaled on a cross. It bothered her so much that she asked the school officials to be excused from chapel, because the image filled her with such sadness that she couldn't even concentrate on her schoolwork.

We were informed that attendance at chapel was mandatory. The end result was that we transferred her to another school, where such images of suffering did not exist.

I often think that Saje's experience as a seven-year-old child is indicative of a larger but identical problem on the planet. Jesus said *I am the resurrection*—the transcendent being of light made of love (God is love) that is in all of us. Yet much of the world's Christian attention is focused on the crucifixion of Jesus—the suffering being who has nails in his hands and feet, a crown of thorns, blood dripping down his face, and a wound in his side. This is an image focusing on the suffering, tormented soul in all of us, which then promotes more suffering and terror. It dwells on the false idea that God is equated with suffering.

I prefer the artistic interpretations of Jesus as the resurrection, filled with love and light, transcending earthly suffering and encouraging all of us to love each other rather than the offerings that depict him as a tortured soul. How different our world might be if we focused on the resurrection, rather than the crucifixion. Collectively, we might live out this mandate and see the eternal resurrected light that truly defines our *I am* nature. We might be taking a giant step toward the idea reflected in the words "On earth as it is in Heaven" (Matthew 6:10).

In reading the scriptures while doing research for this book, I noted that the word *me* when used by Jesus is capitalized or italicized for emphasis. So who was this great teacher referring to when he used words like "without Me you can do nothing," or "No one comes to the Father except through Me"? If he meant Jesus the man who walked among us, then it would make sense to idolize Jesus as the one and only anointed one who has all the powers of God as His only son. Yet in his own words, according to the same scriptures, he reminds us, "It is the Spirit who gives life; the flesh profits nothing. The words that I speak to you are spirit, and they are life" (John 6:63). This point needs your deepest attention.

When Jesus says "Me" or "I am the way," he isn't talking about his bodily self—the man who walks and talks. He is speaking as God, whose name he has told us is I Am. He reminded us that the flesh counts for nothing, so we can presume he is speaking about his own flesh as well. He further confirms this point by saying, "The words that I speak to you are spirit, and they are life."

The person who was Jesus knew that the creative Source of the universe is the words *I am that I am.* He was wise and holy enough to realize that the words *I am* were the *spirit of God* speaking and not the human body comprised of flesh and bones. This is the essential message of this chapter on your highest self. You are God. Jesus later speaks to you in these words: "Most assuredly, I say to you, he who believes in Me, the works that I do he will do also; and greater works than these he will do"(John 14:12).

There is that *Me* again; the same *Me* that is you, when you stay aligned and know that you too can and will do great and greater works when you cast out all doubt about your own divinity and live as you are encouraged to live, not just as a piece of God, but as God Himself. Yes, *you need not consider it robbery to be equal with God.* This is the logical sequence that can and will allow you to change your concept of yourself and recognize your Divine nature, and the fundamental truth that when you become one with your creator, as co-creator you gain all of the powers that are inherent in saying "I am God." Meaning, of course, that God is love.

As Neville so succinctly stated, "It is I AM's concept of itself that determines the form and scenery of its existence. Everything depends upon its attitude toward itself; that which it will not affirm as true of itself cannot awaken in its world."[9]

See if you can accept this logical sequence leading to a new concept of yourself as God altogether:

- God speaks to Moses and announces his name for all future generations to know. *I am that I am.*

- Jesus, some 1,300 years later, acknowledges God as *I am.*

- Jesus reminds us that he too is God with his many *I am the way* pronouncements.

- Jesus tells us that we are all equal with God.

- Jesus assures us that he speaks as spirit and that the flesh counts for nothing.

- Jesus tells us that we too can do all that he does, because we are God also.

- You are God—the I am that I am. Know it and stay in harmony with this Divine *I am* presence.

Perhaps now it doesn't sound so foreign to assert your Divine nature. You might want to start by being careful not to use the words *I am* when describing yourself in any way that isn't congruous with your newly awakened God-realized self.

I return to the poets to sum up that original meeting between Moses and God disguised as a burning bush that resists being consumed:

> *Earth's crammed with heaven,*
> *And every common bush afire with God;*
> *But only he who sees takes off his shoes,*
> *The rest sit round it and pluck blackberries*
>
> — ELIZABETH BARRETT BROWNING

Yes, indeed, Earth's crammed with heaven, and you are Earth, filled to overflow with God. So take off your shoes and respect the holy space that is you.

Three Suggestions

— Become conscious of precisely how you are using the words *I am* in your daily conversations. If whatever follows these two words is not fully aligned with your perception of how the creative Source of the universe would be speaking, then make the correction on the spot. Say to yourself "*I am* the resurrection and the life in thought and feeling." According to *The "I AM" Discourses* of Saint Germain: "It immediately turns all the energy of your Being to the center in the brain which is the source of your Being. You cannot overestimate the Power in this Statement. There is no limit to what you can do with it. It was the Statement that Jesus used most in his most difficult trials."[10]

— Notice how those around you, particularly family and close friends, use and misuse the inherent power of *I am* in their lives. Observe that many people say, "I am weak, poor, depressed, sick, sad, afraid, unlucky," and so on, and they continue to attract that into their life. If they are willing to listen and change, gently remind them that there is no way to attract what they prefer without acknowledging and applying the active presence of God in them. No arguments—just gentle reminders. By observing and teaching the *I am* awareness, you will become more aligned with your highest self.

— Remind yourself often that you have to send the old unworkable fabrications about your highest self out of your life forever. Be able to say "I am God" with pride and assurance that you are not being blasphemous or inappropriate. Believing in that ego-driven idea of God as a malevolent superbeing who plays favorites and is filled with rage if you displease Him is akin to believing in the Easter bunny and praying to that rabbit to solve your problems. Keep uppermost in your thoughts the words of Jesus—"God is love" —and that you are proud to be that all-powerful God yourself.

PART II

THE FIVE WISHES FULFILLED FOUNDATIONS

"Everything which you can conceive and accept is yours! Entertain no doubt. Refuse to accept worry or hurry or fear. That which knows and does everything is inside you and harkens to the slightest whisper."

— UELL STANLEY ANDERSEN

THE FIRST
WISHES FULFILLED
FOUNDATION:

USING YOUR IMAGINATION

*"Imagination is more important than knowledge.
Knowledge is limited. Imagination encircles the world."*

— ALBERT EINSTEIN

While walking down a crowded street in London many years ago, I noticed a window display devoted to the English poet William Blake. There was a quotation on a sign in the window that I read over and over. The words seemed to touch my soul, and I was prompted by an internal calling to write those words on the back of an envelope. Blake's 200-year-old words resonated strongly with me. I had a curious knowing that I'd one day be writing about what he'd had to say.

Fast-forward some ten years later to the day I began writing this chapter about that most mysterious function of our human lives—our imagination. During the morning before settling in to write, I was searching for some tax records in a desk drawer. Unsought, the Blake quote scribbled on the back of an envelope, which had long ago been misplaced, appeared. As I grabbed the ten-year-old envelope, I pondered for a moment how Divine synchronicity is always working, moving the pieces around while our ego believes we are in charge. Here I was, ready to begin writing a chapter on how to use your imagination, and today of all days, these scribbles reappeared after a decade of being "lost." How could I ignore this synchronicity?

So I share these words with you from my spiritual mentor back in the 18th century:

> The tree which moves some to tears of joy is in the eyes of others only a Green thing that stands in the way. Some see Nature all Ridicule and Deformity . . . and some scarce see Nature at all. But to the eyes of the Man of Imagination, Nature is Imagination itself.

The greatest gift you were ever given was the gift of your imagination. Within your magical inner realm is the capacity to have all of your wishes fulfilled. Here in your imagination lies the greatest power you will ever know. It is your domain for creating the life that you desire, and the best part of it is that you are the monarch with all of the inherent powers to rule your world as you desire.

The essence of this great gift is found within another observation made by William Blake, the intuitive poet who lived at the time of the American Revolution. Writing in *The Marriage of Heaven and Hell,* he made this wry comment that is the great secret for living a life of creative manifestation: "What is now proved was once only imagin'd." Allow yourself to contemplate this. As this one line of great wisdom sinks into your consciousness, your imagination will then begin to take over.

Look around you. Everything that you can experience with your senses was once in someone's imagination. This is the great truth that you must come to realize for yourself. In order for something to get into this world where things exist and are *proved*, as Blake says, they must first be placed firmly into your imagination. Without your imagination as the reason for future creations, the process of creativity is halted. You have this great power within you. It is a power that is virtually unlimited, and it has been given to you as your birthright.

Before putting this gift to work, it is crucial for you to know that virtually all spiritual teachings have spoken of the power that Blake comments on in that insightful sentence, "What is now proved was once only imagin'd." In the year that I spent researching and living the Tao for my book *Change Your Thoughts—Change Your Life,* this truth jumped out at me in the lines of the 40th verse of the Tao Te Ching. "Being is born of nonbeing" was Lao-tzu's observation 2,500 years ago. The visible world of being originates in nonbeing. Some 500 years later Jesus would tell his followers, "It is the Spirit who gives life" (John 6:63). I could go on through all of the great spiritual traditions and offer you quote upon quote that states that it is in the invisible formless realm that the originating spark of life begins.

Today, the world of quantum physics confirms that the universe is made of formless (spirit) energy, and that particles (that is, things) do not originate from particles (things). Everything springs from something that is akin to your imagination. You can't touch, taste, see, hear, or smell it. It has no boundaries. You can't prove it with mathematical formulas or scientific verification. Yet we all know that it exists. These invisible thoughts that you have—these ideas that continue to percolate within you, these fanciful images that are always with you—are beyond the scope of science to prove or disprove.

I love this observation made by Max Planck, the father of quantum theory: "Science cannot solve the ultimate mystery of nature. And that is because, in the last analysis, we ourselves are part of nature and, therefore, part of the mystery that we are trying to solve." You simply know that you have an imagination, and that this imagination is the Source of all being. It is up to you to channel and use this magnificent endowment to work in the creation of all that you choose to place in that imagination.

Taking Charge of Your Imagination

My favorite definition of success, which I've cited on numerous occasions, was offered by Henry David Thoreau in the mid-19th century at Walden Pond: "If one advances confidently in the direction of his *dreams,* and endeavors to live the life which he has *imagined,* he will meet with a success unexpected in common hours." I've italicized two words in Thoreau's definition of success—*dreams* and *imagined.*

What Thoreau is saying is so important to you today. Be willing to dream, and imagine yourself becoming all that you wish to be. If you live from those imaginings, the universe will align with you in bringing all that you wish for—and even more than you imagined when you were living at an ordinary level of consciousness, or what Thoreau calls "common hours." Keep in mind this basic axiom—if all that now exists was once imagined, then what you want to exist for you in the future must now be imagined.

You'll see as you read through these foundations for fulfilling your wishes that using your imagination involves more intensity on your part than just imagining an occasional wishful thought. You must first unlearn some of the ways that you've been misusing or squandering the capacity your imagination has for providing you with an unlimited ability to manifest all that you desire. Thoreau called it advancing confidently in the direction of your own dreams. Unfortunately, most of us have learned to do the opposite with our imagination, and instead regularly use it to develop mental habits of advancing in precisely the reverse direction of our highest dreams for ourselves.

In the next chapter I address in depth how to utilize the *I ams* and live from your *I am God* awareness, beginning with your imagination. Recall that *I am God* doesn't refer to your body in any way. It refers to the birthless, deathless, changeless spirit that remains in all the changing forms your body takes every moment of your temporary life here on Earth.

It is important that you recognize a few of the *imagination* missteps that will block you from fulfilling your unique desires. Remember that your imagination is yours and yours alone. You have the inborn capacity to use it in any way that you choose. No one else is responsible for *your* imagination. Anything placed in your imagination and held there ultimately becomes your reality.

Nikos Kazantzakis reinforces this idea by giving these words to his fanciful character Zorba (in his book *Zorba the Greek*), who always lived his life to the fullest: "By believing passionately in something that does not yet exist we create it. The nonexistent is whatever we have not sufficiently desired." This is the power of your imagination when what you desire is imagined sufficiently to make it your reality. Don't diminish this great gift by using it in a way that is antithetical to its *I am God* original nature.

Perhaps the most common misuse of imagination is stressing what you *don't want* for yourself. This is the largest category of misusing imagination. Start paying attention to general conversation, and you will be astounded by how incredibly prevalent it is. Imagining that finds expression in phrases like, *I don't deserve prosperity, I am always so unlucky, Things never work out for me,* and *I am unhealthy and cannot be healed,* are the kind of ideas that may have been entertained since childhood. Highly functioning self-actualized people simply *never* imagine what it is that they *don't* wish to have as their reality.

Begin noticing and being careful about keeping your imagination free of thoughts that you do not wish to materialize. Instead, initiate a practice of filling your creative thoughts to overflow with ideas and wishes that you fully intend to manifest. Honor your imaginings regardless of others seeing them as crazy or impossible. Recall the words of Kazantzakis and passionately believe in that which is in your imagination and which does not yet exist on the physical plane.

Some Rules for a Healthy Imagination

— **Rule number one** is: *never* place into your imagination any thought that you would not want to materialize.

— **Rule number two** is of equal importance: never allow your imagination to be contaminated by ideas about how your life *used to be.* You need faith in your power to make the nonexistent your reality. Just because you haven't experienced the magic of the non-existent appearing in your daily life is no reason to poison your imagination with the thoughts that got you where you are now or have been for most of your life. *I can't help it, I've always been that way* are statements indicating how you've used your imagination in the past. These lead back to the ordinary level of awareness that I wrote about in the first chapter. Now you must be willing to change your concept of yourself, and you cannot do that by hanging on to those old ideas that once were your truths—those truths have kept you from achieving the complete fulfillment of your dreams.

Your imagination can undergo a complete overhaul. Replace the old ideas of *I've always been this way, It's my nature, It's the only thing I've ever known,* with *I am God, I am capable, I am strong, I am wealthy, I am healthy, I am happy*—or to use the words of Saint Germain, "'I AM the Conquering Presence'! I command this 'I AM Presence' to govern perfectly my mind, home, affairs and world."[11] Use your imagination for the fulfillment of all your God-realized and God-aligned wishes. Expand your imagination beyond the concept of yourself that limits you to ordinary consciousness.

— **Rule number three** is a strong reminder to you that your imagination is yours and yours alone. It is a vast, boundaryless realm within you that no one else has access to. No one can peer into your imagination and place things in there that they prefer for you, nor can they extract any ideas that are percolating in that grand imagination of yours. Your imagination is your own fertile field for growing any seedlings that you choose to plant for a future harvest. This rule advises you to never allow someone else's ideas about what is possible or impossible for you, how you should be thinking, or who you should be—or anything else—to occupy your imagination. Regularly inventory the thoughts in your imagination. Notice how many of those ideas were originally suggested by well-meaning *others,* dating all the way back to your early childhood, up to and including today.

You may have been told that you have always been a dreamer, as if this were a fault. I can speak here from experience. Family, friends, teachers, and even advisors frequently disparaged ideas that burned brightly in my imagination. I often heard comments such as, "Wayne, you're such a dreamer. Get real. You are never going to make it as a writer, or a television performer, or a movie personality. Be realistic—we know what's best for you."

When I was being discharged from the Navy at the age of 22, my superiors warned me that starting college at my "advanced age" was loaded with uncertainty, particularly since I had no higher education experience, and I would be competing with younger recent high school graduates. Since I already had a skill as a cryptographer in the Navy, they advised me to pursue what they felt was best for me. But I had a dream—an imagination filled with the idea of teaching, writing, and speaking to large audiences. I saw myself onstage. I saw myself as a prominent author. And this vision could not and would not be sabotaged by someone else's vision of what I should or could become.

As a young boy in a foster home, I almost always ignored other people's ideas about what I should be thinking or doing—I simply was indifferent to their opinions regarding what I could imagine for myself. I have carried this kind of inner discipline regarding my own imagination with clarity, refusing to allow external opinions to cancel or diminish what for me was hallowed ground.

Recently, others advised me that acting in a movie was not sensible for me as a 68-year-old man with no acting experience. I once again remembered to hang the Do Not Disturb sign at the entrance to my imagination, and proceeded to take acting lessons and adopt the *self-enforced* regimen that allowed me to create a movie. It is a product that fills me with pride today—all because I have diligently practiced rule three.

Never, and I mean *never,* allow anyone else's ideas of who you can or can't become to sully *your dream* or pollute your imagination. This is your territory, and a Keep Out sign is a great thing to erect at all entrances to your imagination.

Generally speaking, the viewpoints of other people regarding how you should occupy your imagination involve their own self-interest. My naval superiors were really not so concerned with my own ideas about becoming a teacher, writer, and public speaker; they saw a promising naval officer in the making and wanted me to reenlist to help fulfill their own objectives and quotas. And so it is with most well-meaning, self-appointed life coaches who tell you how you should be thinking about your future. Often they're trying to fulfill their wishes of needing to feel superior by advising others what to do. Frequently the inclination to meddle in your imagination is a way to get something for themselves by persuading you of the folly of your dreams. Enlist only those (including yourself) who are primarily interested in what you see or hear in your imagination about your life.

— **Rule number four** may surprise you. It concerns what you don't want to let monopolize your imagination. Do not let your imagination be restricted to the current conditions of your life, or what I call "being obsessed with what is." Your imagination is unlimited, and if you've opted for an ordinary level of living, it is tempting to stay in "what is" rather than what you unabashedly intend to manifest for yourself. Keep reminding yourself that everything that you've believed has gotten you to precisely the point where you are now. This is a rather persistent theme in this book, so it bears repeating here: If you want to elevate your life and become a manifester, then you have to change what you've believed to be true about yourself that has landed you where you are. The sentiments of *This is reality, This is just the way things are, There is nothing that I can do to change what is,* and the like are pernicious thoughts that will taint and defile your great gift of *I am that I am,* which is your Divine inheritance from your creator.

Just as growth isn't possible if one continues doing things exactly the same today as yesterday and tomorrow, so is your imagination charged with the same challenge. In your imagination, you can replace the thought of *I will one day be in a better place,* with *I am already in my mind where I intend to be.* This may sound irrational because you are accustomed to evaluating your life on the basis of what your senses tell you is your reality. After reading Chapter Five and familiarizing yourself with this imaginative way of approaching your life, you will be able to integrate this idea in your own special way.

As a brief teaser here, I ask you to remember that God didn't say to Moses, "My name is *I will be,*" because to do so would be to admit that God is lacking something now that he will ultimately become. He said, *"I am that I am."* You too have been bestowed with the *I am* legacy. You can make the choice to reprogram your imagination to take you where you intend to be: in the now. Creation originates in the world of Spirit—or, to say it differently, your imagination is the Source of all that has yet to manifest for you. By staying only with what your senses tell you is your reality, you place a barrier to letting your imagination create all that you wish, all that you desire. Your imagination is unlimited. What is today, is restricted by just that: what is today.

Albert Einstein made this astute observation: "Logic will get you from A to B. Imagination will take you everywhere." Your logic—that is, the facts that you've accepted as true—have gotten you to point B. Now you're going to *reprogram* your imagination to take you everywhere—*everywhere* that you are brave enough to envision for yourself.

In the quotation on success that I shared with you earlier, Henry David Thoreau's last sentence is fitting for this first foundation for a wishes fulfilled life: "[You] will meet with a success unexpected in common hours." Thoreau suggests that the universe will begin to conspire with you to fulfill your wishes. It isn't just your imagination that will bring you what you desire—it's the fact that you're realigned with the *I am that I am*. When you become it in your mind, you gain the same powers as that which you are now casting your lot with: God or the Tao.

Your Highest Self and Your Imagination

The essence of you—the you who is a spiritual being having a temporary human experience—is cultivated in your imagination. The *I am that I am*—that is, the you that is God—is impervious to the senses. There's an invisible realm within and around you that is you, and your imagination is your key to realigning with this *I am* presence, which Einstein said "will take you everywhere." Within this realm, guidance is always available when *(1) You are open to it,* and most important, *(2) You are aligned in body, mind, and spirit.* This means living in harmony with your own personal dharma, feeling on purpose living the life you were intended to live, and feeling the presence of your highest self at work.

This guidance comes in ways that you don't experience when your life is off purpose, or when you prefer negative emotions such as fear, anxiety, worry, hatred, sadness, and the like. Each of these dubious emotional states takes you away from your God-realized self. Remember, God's name is *I am,* so how could God say, "I am afraid, I am worried, I am angry, I am sad," and still be God?! Impossible, because God is love and God is oneness. In order for God to be afraid, worried, angry, or sad, She'd have to divide Herself and have something other than self to fear, worry about, hate, or be sad toward. This would make God two: that is, Herself as well as an other to feel gloomy or angry toward, and God cannot do this and still be God.

So it is with you as well. Every time you put a non-God descriptor after *I am,* you negate your Divine nature. The words *I am* are your sacred identification as God—your highest self. Take care how you use this term because saying anything after *I am* that's incongruent with God is really taking the Lord's name in vain! Practice using imagination to define yourself only in ways that

are compatible with your highest self, and the universe will supply the happiness, love, and success that you previously imagined
eluding you. This is the meaning of Thoreau's statement "meet
with a success unexpected in common hours." *Common hours* are
the times you spend in *ordinary awareness,* unaware of the nature
of your God-realized being. I emphasize this based on my own
experience.

As I proceed through my seventies, I'm beginning to recognize
more readily the relationship between my conscious invitation to
the God within me, and what the universe has in store for me. It
is simply a sacred imperative for me to live from the knowing that
I am God in the truest sense of the word. The result is being fully
aligned with my own dharma in ways that often appear not to
be connected. Carl Jung called this phenomenon *synchronicity*—
a collaboration with fate that seems to take place with strange and
wonderful "coincidences" happening.

There's a feeling of invisible beings taking the reins of my life
in a profound way. I can feel them, and they make themselves
known to me in a variety of ways that I once would have labeled
far-fetched and impossible. The presence of beings, including
those who have passed on, has become my reality. These angelic
beings steer me in ways that keep me aligned with my dharma
and with my highest self. I feel I'm in a new state of awareness,
rather than being directed by unseen beings. Then I see how I'm
being influenced while still acting from my own treasured free
will. A recent example of this comes to mind.

I was aware on my evening walk that I was taking a slightly
different route as I turned in a different direction than was normal for me. After purchasing some food to take home, I chose to
return home along a route I'd never taken before. On the way I
noticed a fountain and decided to stop for a few moments. Then
as I walked along a path in total darkness, a man called out my
name. Because I had done all of these new things, I was aligned
with someone who recognized me even in total darkness.

We chatted, and I invited this man and his wife and their two
small children into my home. Michael and Angela were on Maui

to commemorate the death nine years earlier of their two-and-a-half-year-old daughter. We talked about their loss, and Angela said that she felt her first child's presence every day. She described it as a feeling of almost giddy joyfulness that permeated her daily life. Angela *knew* that her daughter's passing was a Divine experience, and that her angelic daughter was with her family at all times and also attempting to teach Angela something that remained elusive but exciting to her.

How many unplanned moves did I take in order for us to meet and share an evening discussing just what I am writing about today? Was I in charge or was I being guided? Were Michael and Angela also being guided to that spot for this encounter to take place? I did not feel as if I was being steered—what happened was that I was *aware* just for a fleeting moment. I proceeded to let myself be guided without any sense of listening to extraterrestrial voices, anticipating something grand was going to show up. It was only later that I looked back and saw how all my nonroutine moves were guidance of some kind that allowed that evening meeting to occur. What transpired in that meeting is what prompted me to tell this story, because it illustrates living from the place of allowing imagination to freely function. Something seems to kick in and generate circumstances to fulfill our wishes.

During our evening together I told Michael and Angela about my experience of an orb (an opaque circular feature that appears unexpectedly in photographs) appearing on my left shoulder in a photo while I was giving a lecture. The woman who took the photograph, Linda Millek, had this tiny mark expanded, revealing a collection of what looked like human faces right there with me as I was delivering a speech on *The "I AM" Discourses*. It turns out that Linda's only son had passed away some 18 years earlier, and he was communicating with her using *I Am* as his channeled calling. Linda has thousands of photos of orbs that she picks up on her camera. She feels her son's presence in orbs that appear majestically in a variety of forms. She is in the process of having her son help to reveal to her what these appearances mean.

Linda took several photos of me on the island of St. Maarten, and these megaphone-shaped orbs were visible on both my left hip and right side. (See photo insert.) The shapes are identical to those that appear on her photographs taken from her bedroom window in Michigan where her son once lived. Linda has absolutely no doubt about the presence of these orbs, at the same time she is in the process of learning what their presence means, and how to best use this information in the fulfillment of a higher calling.

This subject of orbs and their purpose is fascinating. I've just completed my first reading of a book by Dr. Klaus and Gundi Heinemann called *Orbs: Their Mission and Messages of Hope*, complete with 65 color photos of these rather mystical invisible critters, with convincing commentary and visual evidence to convert the skeptic. I have the photos of these orbs and their highly enlarged images in my home, and I have been astonished to discover how my feelings of not being alone in this new *I am* journey are being verified not only with my increased awareness, but with photographic evidence as well.

As Linda said to me when we reviewed her videos of the orbs, as well as a mountain of photographs containing orbs and her transmissions from her son, "It's like following these spiritual bread crumbs. Suddenly all of the crazy things that are happening to you begin to make sense." I have never met anyone who was more totally convinced that she was receiving guidance from her loved one on the other side and that these orbs and their fascinating shapes and human faces have powerful messages of hope for all of us.

During my "chance" encounter with Michael and Angela, I felt compelled to tell them about my recent orb experience, particularly after Angela told me how profoundly she felt her daughter's presence, even though she had been dead for nine years. I showed them the photos and told them how much of what was now showing up in my life was (to quote Thoreau again) "unexpected in common hours." I learned that they had hundreds of photos with orbs that they interpreted as their daughter's mysterious appearance showing up to teach us all something.

Perhaps all of the things that aligned in order for me to meet this family occurred so that someone reading this book would read these words and consider the possibility of guidance being available from another realm—and commit to using their imagination in a new way. That someone may be you. Let your imagination explore your invisible realm in a way that will allow this new energy to permeate your life. Move to a place within yourself where *Wishes Fulfilled* is a new way of being rather than just the title of a book.

C. Norman Shealy, M.D., Ph.D., is a distinguished professor and university president who has this to say concerning orbs:

> When Anthonie van Leeuwenhoek used the microscope to introduce us to bacteria and microorganisms, he opened another dimension. Now we are being introduced to yet another mysterious dimension, that of the orb. I expect this new experience will yield an even more exciting world than did the microscope. Here you will find unequaled beauty and mystery!

"Unequaled beauty and mystery," indeed! And I'd add, "Surreal evidence that intelligent guidance is sitting right there on your shoulder!" Allow yourself to follow your dreams and encourage your imagination by having *a mind that is open to everything and attached to nothing.*

You will discover the bewildering world of synchronicity blossoming before your eyes when your imagination encapsulates your intention to manifest for yourself and others. This is because you align with the powerful God force that created form from spirit. As you've heard many times—*with God, all things are possible.* This Divine force awaits your imaginative energy. It can quite easily send the right people at the right time. Your highest self says, *Of course!* though it appears mystifying at the time. This happens naturally when you turn your attention and imagination to God within. A sacred sense of rightness lets you know you're evolving to a new level rather than living through your ego's limited ideas of who you are and what you can become.

The presence of angels to lift you up when you are down, to rearrange things so that what seems like enigmatic unexplainable circumstances is reality. Healing that seems blessedly baffling, the confounding showing up of financial aid at precisely the moment it is needed, the perplexing arrival of a book containing the information you've been desiring but has been eluding you, the unexpected phone call that gives you the answers you've been seeking, the sudden healthy shift in behavior of a loved one who was seemingly lost—the possibilities are endless. Congruency with the creative Source of the universe in your own Divine imagination makes what you wish for not only probable but dead-on inevitable.

I want to again refer to my spiritual soul mate Neville, the inspiration for me to write this book. He directs us to Saint Paul's letter to the people of Ephesus: "Now to Him who is able to do exceedingly abundantly above all that we ask or think, according to the power that works in us" (Ephesians 3:20). Neville suggests that the *Him* in this passage, who is able to do more than we can think or ask, is *imagination—the power that works in us*. He states:

> Understanding imagination to be HIM that is able to do all you ask, and attention to be the power by which you create your world, you can now build your ideal world. Imagine yourself to be the ideal you dream of and desire. Remain attentive to this imagined state, and as fast as you completely feel that you are already this ideal it will manifest itself as *reality* in your world.[12]

In the chapters that follow, I present at length the significance of feeling that you are already this ideal and the importance of the word *attention* in manifesting your new reality. As I close this chapter on the relevance and utter momentousness of your imagination keep in mind Saint Paul's words. There is a power in the universe that is able to go way beyond all that you could ever ask or even think, and it *works in you*. What else could this be other than your own imagination? Stay in a state of grace and gratitude for this resplendent gift that is always yours to do with as you choose.

Three Suggestions

— Become adamant about your imagination being your private sacred inner space. Be clear that no one is ever allowed to besmirch it in any way. Speak to your imagination with reverence. Pay homage to it. Stay in a constant state of gratitude for this beautiful inner sanctum that is your highest *I am that I am,* which you share with the creative Source of the entire universe.

— Place no limits on what you allow yourself to imagine, and store those exalted ideas in a private place within you that no one is capable of sullying or discouraging. Place a Keep Out sign at the edge of your imagination to remind yourself that this is a private venue.

— Invite the mysterious unseen world of Spirit to guide you. Create an atmosphere of allowing it in without pushing it. Recall Saint Paul's advice: "That which is seen, hath not come from that which doth appear." Funny language perhaps for us in the 21st century, but nevertheless, a powerful message to keep in your heart. It all comes from Spirit, and your own imagination is that very Spirit if you stay aligned with the unseen.

THE SECOND WISHES FULFILLED FOUNDATION:

LIVE FROM THE END

*"In the presence of Him whom he believed—
God, who gives life to the dead and calls those
things which do not exist as though they did."*

— ROMANS 4:17

You might find that this second foundation for a wishes ful-filled life is the most troublesome and unconventional idea that you tackle. If you find that this is true for you, I encourage you to rustle up all the determination you are capable of. You are going to begin retraining your imagination so that it accepts the idea that anything placed there isn't for a future experience, but *represents your reality, right here, right now.* You are being asked to put your five senses into a lockbox so that they can't persuade you that you are ignoring what *they* perceive as reality. You are stepping into a new dimension, the unaccustomed reality that Saint Paul speaks of in his letters to the people of Rome in Romans 4:17, cited above.

Keep in mind a fundamental axiom of this book, the strong *knowing* I described in Chapter Three and stress throughout this book: *We are all God.* "Is it not written in your law, 'I said, "You are gods"'?" (John 10:34) was the response of Jesus when he was about to be stoned. "For a good work we do not stone You, but for blasphemy, and because You, being a man, make Yourself God" (John 10:33). I quote this to remind you that it is not me, some crazy 21st-century writer, saying these words; they are directly out of the scriptures.

Now simply review the line Saint Paul speaks in Romans 4:17: "and calls those things which do not exist as though they did." This is how God works. Your imagination, when aligned with the highest principles of your highest self, is God at work. You can make your imagination a place where you absolutely "call things" as you insist that they be, even though they may not have appeared in the third dimension as reported by your five senses. This is where you must learn to trust, think, and *live from* rather than in *anticipation of.* Hence the title of this chapter: "Live from the End."

As I sit here writing, there's a book with a beautiful jacket taped around it. The jacket is exactly the same as the cover of the book you are now reading, titled *Wishes Fulfilled.* I'm only one-third of the way through the actual writing of this book, yet I see the completed book every day when I approach my sacred writing space. This is a practice I've maintained for many years. As I'm in the process of writing, I see the finished book every day, both in my imagination and in its symbolic representation.

My imagination is where my thoughts are the thoughts of God, and thus I am God creating what I know is already present. I am "calling that which does not exist as though it did." Knowing and feeling this means nothing can dissuade me from this creative force in my imagination. There's no fear about completing some awesome undertaking of writing a book—it's already complete in my mind. I simply allow the energy to flow into me, through my

Here I am speaking to a large audience in Vancouver, B.C., at Hay House's I Can Do It! event.

Speaking to the "Experiencing the Miraculous" audience in Dubrovnik, Croatia. Note the large orb on my left hip.

With two of my daughters, Serena and Saje, in Lourdes, France.

Another orb appearance in Lourdes, with Serena and Saje.

I spoke to the "Experiencing the Miraculous" group in this church in Assisi, below the likeness of Jesus.

With Nicollette and her mother, Linda. The left side of Nicollette's face was paralyzed before she received wishes fulfilled counseling and cranio-sacral therapy.

Nicollette, paralysis-free, and with an orb on her left shoulder.

A painting of Jesus in Rayna Piskova's hotel room, where she was recovering from surgery from John of God in Brazil.

The identical painting of Jesus, on a candle purchased by my daughter Saje in Brazil. I looked at this every day while writing this book and recuperating from remote surgery from John of God.

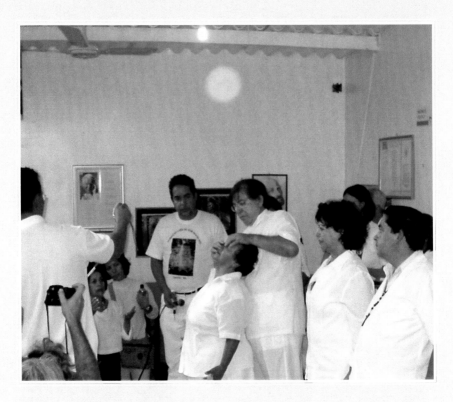

John of God performing "visible interventions" in Brazil. *(Reproduced from* <u>Orbs</u> *by Klaus Heinemann, Ph.D., and Gundi Heinemann. Used with permission.)*

Megaphone-shaped orbs in
Linda Millek's bedroom.

On a Hay House
cruise to Saint Maarten.
Note the identical
megaphone-shaped orb
on my left hip . . .

. . . and on my right hip.

Orbs surrounding my daughters in Maui.

Orbs fill the room in Vernon, B.C., where I am autographing books during a break in my lecture.

Speaking at the "Celebrate Your Life" conference in Phoenix, Arizona. Note the presence of blue orbs, which I recently learned are especially significant, since blue represents "Master Teacher energy."

heart, and onto the pages. I recently made the following observation concerning the topic "Are You a Writer?" on my website: "Stop judging and get out of your own way. I always tell audiences when I talk about writing: Writing isn't something I do; writing is something that I am. I am writing—it's just an expression of me."

Notice the words *I am* (the name of God for all generations to come), which were told to Moses in the Torah. Begin to focus your attention on words that follow the sacred name of God—your highest self—that is, *I am*. Begin to recognize the power of your creative imagination to fulfill wishes with *I am*.

The Power of Your Imagination

Figuratively tattoo these words of Neville onto your forehead. In other words, memorize them, and repeat them to yourself every time you look into the mirror:

> Disregard appearances, conditions, in fact all evidence of your senses that deny the fulfillment of your desire. Rest in the assumption that you are already what you want to be, for in that determined assumption you and your Infinite Being are merged in creative unity, *and with your Infinite Being (God) all things are possible.* God never fails.[13]

Your concept of yourself is being replaced by a new concept of yourself.

A new self-concept begins with you placing it in your imagination and living from this new perspective. You can count on your five senses to attempt to convince you that you should pay homage only to them and treat your imagination as unimportant and illusory. But that doesn't mean that you have to allow them to usurp your new concept of yourself.

Right now, in this moment, you can practice this. Say aloud or to yourself, *By placing new I ams into my imagination, my future dream is a present fact.* Repeat the statement a few times. Can you feel your ego resisting? Which of your five senses is most adamantly annoyed? Notice and repeat. This new concept of yourself as

God, or at least as a spark of God, asks you to think like God, Who "calls those things which do not exist as though they did."

Here, you are creating an ideal of what you want to be and assuming that you already are that person. This is what Neville calls the Law of Assumption, and he states emphatically, "If this assumption is persisted in until it becomes your dominant feeling, the attainment of your ideal is inevitable."[14]

Remind yourself that your imagination is yours to use as you decide, and that everything you wish to manifest into your physical world must first be placed firmly in your imagination in order to grow. Let Neville's words guide you:

> Therefore, to incarnate a new and greater value of yourself, you must assume that you already are what you want to be and then live by faith in this assumption—which is not yet incarnate in the body of your life—in confidence that this new value or state of consciousness will become incarnated through your absolute fidelity to the assumption that you are that which you desire to be.[15]

This is a total transformation of your entire being.

Within your imagination, you can conceive thoughts of what you want as already here—prior to their birth in form in the sensory world. This means that your thoughts aren't along the lines of: *I will be. I hope it works out. I'm praying for good results.* Instead, you say to yourself: *I am—acknowledging the I am presence as God dwelling in me.* Then your mind as that *I am* presence will become the dominant creative feature in your life. This generative force will gently assert its authentic creativity and power as you conceive it, and in the process replace a dependency on your physical and intellectual abilities. Your renewed reality does not rely exclusively on those five senses that keep you attached to the false beliefs that you are your body or its possessions, achievements, and reputation.

You've already discovered that the different bodies you've occupied throughout your life so far no longer exist for your senses to experience. Now you can choose to consciously participate in this nonsensory supreme reality—your imagination—where you assume your future dream to be a present fact and live from this new awareness. This isn't pretending or fooling yourself, it is inviting your spirit rather than your physical form to generate the creative essence of your reality. It's what it means to *transform* your life.

The word *transformation* has the word *form* right smack in the middle, preceded by *trans*—meaning going beyond form. Live from the place that will indeed take you way beyond the limits of your seemingly limited life. Explore imagination, which is the Source of all being or physical reality.

Throughout my life I've often been called excessively persistent and even obsessive in going after what I wish to fulfill. The truth is that I have within me a very powerful knowing that when I place something into my imagination, it is already a fact for me. I just don't seem to have the capacity to erase from my mind what it is that is already my reality. For instance, earlier in my life when I applied to a doctoral program, I already saw myself with a doctorate, although I hadn't taken even one course toward that degree. When I was told that nine out of ten doctoral students do not receive their degree because they cannot complete the vigorous requirements of writing a dissertation, I knew that this did not apply to me, because I was already a doctor in my imagination. I persistently acted as if my dream were a present fact.

I've had this same kind of "thinking from the end" in every phase of my professional career. As a young boy I saw myself on television shows and vehemently held this inner picture in my imagination, ignoring a lot of naysayers! And these imaginings ultimately were taken from my mind, where they were real, to the material world, where my senses finally caught up and confirmed them as truths.

The facts are, for me, that a picture in my imagination is already my reality. I live from this perspective, and nothing can dissuade me from this stance because I am not *hoping* to get someplace else. *I am already there.* I just don't know how to erase what I am living in my imagination, even if the whole world attempts to persuade me of the folly of my dreams. This is a mind-set you can choose to embrace.

Let go of all doubt, forget about the *when*. It will develop into a material fact on Divine time. Forget about the *how*. Live it inwardly. This is a great power that you possess if you are willing to claim it as your own.

I cannot emphasize strongly enough how vital it is for you to claim this inherent power of God and use it for manifesting the life you desire. Be obstinate regarding this idea. Hold your vision relentlessly, and more than that—live each day as if that idea you have in your imagination is in fact your reality. In *The "I AM" Discourses*, Saint Germain repeatedly reminds us that we are the master and have dominion in our lives; once this is part of your awareness, you can access the energy, power, and intelligence of the mighty *I am* presence, which is your very birthright. This *I am* presence is always with you.

Moving from I Am Not to I Am!

Throughout life you've been through a conditioning process that's created a mind-set overflowing with *I am not*s. As a schoolchild with a less than satisfactory grade on your report card, you thought to yourself, *I am not smart*. You place anywhere other than number one and say, *I am not talented*. You feel criticized and believe that *I am not good*. You look in the mirror and compare yourself to a glamorous movie idol or homecoming queen and tell yourself, *I am not attractive*. Your relationship fractures and you think, *I am unloved* or *I am unworthy*. These, and many more like them, are repeated throughout your developmental years and into adulthood, and become your core defining self-concept.

You are reading this book because you wish to elevate your life to heights way beyond *ordinary*. You are endeavoring to adopt new truths that are harmonious with your higher and highest self. Now is the perfect time for you to begin discovering the God within you and yourself as God, and to expand your self-concept.

I applaud you! Your self-concept is everything that you believe to be true about yourself.

Overcoming this *I am not* mentality begins with trusting your inner world of spirit. There are no boundaries restricting your inner world. But your worldview and your self-concept in the outer world are defined by your five senses. The outer world is always changing, which, by our previous definition, means it is not real. This awareness could lead to you experiencing a majestic wake-up call right here, right now.

How does it feel to realize that most of what you believe about yourself and your limitations is based on an illusion—a well-intentioned illusion handed to you by people in bodies that no longer exist, in a time that has passed? Much of your self-concept is a fiction based on beliefs that are untrue and contained no veracity when you were first exposed to them. This is exquisitely detailed by Anita Moorjani, who had a near-death experience (NDE) that challenged all her previous self-concepts about who and what she was. Her story illustrates that there's another dimension where you can become one with God and create miracles in your everyday life.

Anita had Hodgkin's lymphoma throughout her body. Her organs were shutting down, and she was told that she had less than 36 hours to live. On the website for the Near Death Experience Research Foundation (**nderf.org**), she relates: "Then I actually 'crossed over' to another dimension, where I was engulfed in a total feeling of love. I also experienced extreme clarity of why I had the cancer, why I had come into this life in the first place, what role everyone in my family played in my life in the grand scheme of things, and generally how life works."

While in her NDE state, Anita was shown that everything going on in our lives is dependent on this energy around us, created by us. Nothing is solid—we are the creators of our surroundings and life conditions depending on how we use this energy. Our physical bodies become sick because of the energetic level at which we live. As Anita reports, "I realized that if I went back, it would be with a very healthy energy. Then the physical body would catch up to the energetic conditions very quickly and permanently. I was given the understanding that this applies to anything, not only illnesses."

Anita was given the opportunity to return to her cancer-ravaged body. Astoundingly, four days after her NDE, her body showed almost no signs of cancer. Essentially, this woman discovered the *I am God* lesson of this book, as well as the great message of Jesus that I've detailed in the previous chapters.

I made contact with Anita and encouraged her to write her own book and share her remarkable story with the world. Her book, titled *Dying to Be Me,* is an incredibly inspiring and compelling account of her experience. Anita's physical body, with billions of cancer cells, went from being at death's door to being cancer-free following her NDE. She has so much to share with us, and I am proud to have written the Foreword to her book.

Anita realized that the seemingly solid world that our senses offer us is an illusion. She changed the outcome of test results and concluded that we can change anything by changing our energy, which we create with our thoughts. For her, this included a *reality* called cancer because a shift in consciousness made it disappear. "From what I saw, it looked like we are energy first, and physical is only a result of expressing our energy," she says. "And we can change our physical reality if we change our energy." This is what your declaration of *I am God* can be for you. God is not physical, it is energy, and this Divine energy is not like the material-world energy that your senses report to you.

Anita reported that she experienced a profound awareness that everything and everyone are interconnected—there is no separation. All she had to do to heal her physical body was to merge into God-consciousness and be perfect love: "I felt one with everything. I felt a connection with every living thing. And it felt like the whole universe is within me." She reports that time and space felt very different in that dimension. "It doesn't feel linear, like it does here. It felt like everything was happening simultaneously."

Anita came to find that even past lives are not past—the words that best describe them are *parallel lives,* because there is no time and no separation. That idea is something that our senses find next to impossible to comprehend because we *think linear*—cause and effect, before and after. For Anita there was only love, and it was an all-consuming love that she described as constructing the entire world: "I was also flooded in all-encompassing, unconditionally loving energy. . . . This universal energy is there for us no matter who or what we are. I felt amazingly powerful and magnificent."

The world that Anita experienced while in her NDE is also your world. It requires making a shift to the true understanding of what the words *I am* signify to you. Live from the perspective that *all things are possible,* planted firmly in the depths of your imagination. The more you believe in your own Divine nature, the more it starts to become real for you.

Anita's almost instantaneous healing from an imminent death prognosis taught her that our highest self is unconditional love—no separation, no time, no judgment. As she puts it, "Whatever you believe, you will find that you are correct." Just think of the importance of living from this perspective now, rather than hoping it will become your reality sometime in the future, or after your body dies.

Living from the *I am God* awareness necessitates knowing that you are one with transcendent unconditional love. This awareness attracts to your life everything that confirms this belief about yourself. Here you are ignoring what your senses preach to you, and after the words *I am,* you are placing the word *magnificent.*

To quote Anita, as she explains what she learned from this amazing NDE: "When you realize your own magnificence, you will only attract magnificence into your life," and "If you believe in things like 'like attracts like,' then the absolute best way to attract what's best for you is to love yourself to the point where you are filled with love, and will only attract to your life everything that confirms this belief about yourself. It's actually very simple, really."

Anita entered the realm of God-realization and lived from there while in her NDE. Yet she also returned to a healthy body after her organs had shut down, and the prognosis was imminent death. She *is love* rather than *loving*. Being love requires no action; it is simply loving yourself and your magnificence so totally that it overflows to all others.

Remember these words that Jesus spoke: "God is love, and he who abides in love abides in God, and God in him." Your *I am* for this is simply *I am Love*. Live from this awareness, rather than the expectation that someday you'll arrive there. You will then capture the quintessence of this second wishes fulfilled foundation. I bring Anita's experience to you here because I was floored by the descriptions she offered concerning this great feeling of being bathed in unconditional love, and this is why I sought her out to write her own story for the world to hear.

I want to bring to your attention one final observation she made about the concept of being in the state of *God-realization.* There is no *there*—it's all just being—so there is no *being here,* because *here* implies the existence of *there.*

As Anita writes: "When we 'pursue' externally, we seem to see the world as being competitive and limited, and we use external measures to judge our achievements. To me, herein lies the illusion. There is no limited supply of 'beingness.' We seem to measure our 'beingness' by the achievement of goals. I don't, and neither do most people who are happy. My point is to shift your views. See the magnificence in your being whether you are rich, or poor, physically impaired or not, with the one you love, or not, and so on. I am now just focused on being, and am now the creator of my life—that is, the artist of my life."

Apropos of the message of this chapter, Anita concludes, "The only thing you need to learn is that you already *are* what you are seeking to attain."

I am inviting you to live this way, first in your imagination— *be it.* Then live your life in the way Saint Paul suggests, treating those things which do not exist as though they did, and surely they will become your reality.

94

Your Reconstructed I Ams

Run through as large an inventory as you can of the things that you would like to define your life. Then make the shift in your imagination from an *I am not* or *I am hoping to become* to *I am.* You want what follows *I am* to be congruent with your highest self, which is God. Beginning with your inner dialogue, simply change the words that define your concept of yourself. Don't discuss what you're doing, because involving others in your *I ams* invites their ego to assert its self-importance. Redefine your self-concept by choosing the words that you opt to place into your imagination. Try this rewording of your inner world as a beginning step to accessing the assistance of your higher self and fulfilling your desires.

In the book of Joel, the Lord's advice is in harmony with what I'm writing in this chapter: "Let the weak say, 'I am strong'" (Joel 3:10). It is truly as simple as these seven words from the Bible advise. If you say, "I am weak," you defile the name of God that is your highest self. How is it possible for the creative Source of the universe, the Source energy responsible for creating worlds, to say, "I am weak"?

As I've quoted previously, Jesus said, "Is it not written in your law, 'I said, "You are gods"'?" So how can you, as you now operate in your life from your highest self, ever even think such a thought as *I am weak,* let alone define yourself in such a blasphemous manner? By thinking *I am strong,* you place in your imagination the tools you need to achieve your pronouncements, and you align with the Source of all, with strength instead of weakness. Align yourself so as to synchronistically invite the guidance that is unavailable when you declare, "I am weak."

Instead of *I am incapable of getting a job,* shift to *I am capable.* Similarly, replace proclamations of *I am not able to live in peace* with *I am peace. I am unlucky in love* is replaced by *I am love. I am unworthy of happiness* becomes *I am happiness.* The words *I am,* which you consistently use to define who you are and what you are capable of, are holy expressions for the name of God—the highest aspect of yourself. Break lifelong habits of unwittingly besmirching this holy name. Discontinue using pejorative labels to cast aspersions on your holy self.

One of the many great lessons of *The "I AM" Discourses* is to always make your very first consideration to your Divine self. In fact, adoration to it will allow you to rise to previously unimagined heights. You must make your outer self accept the unlimited power of your inner presence.

Expanding Your Inner Presence

It is impossible for me to overstate the significance of using these two words *I am.* They have transformative energy to guide and direct the highest power in the universe, revealing you as a God-realized being. The next four chapters explore in detail how to manifest a wishes fulfilled life. *This* chapter emphasizes training yourself to become comfortable with recognizing your tendency to think and say *I am not* or *I hope to be,* and replacing it with *I am.* Neville spoke of it this way: "By creating an ideal in your mind, you can identify yourself with it until you become one and the same with the ideal, thereby transforming yourself into it."[16]

It matters not how long you've been stuck in a pattern that's kept you from fulfilling your highest ideal of yourself. By shifting so that you restate who you are in your imagination and choosing to live from this perspective, you will, as Neville suggests, achieve that transformation. This is true whether you've been a drug addict, a chronic stutterer, enmeshed in poverty, riddled with illness, chronically lazy, unlucky in love, intellectually inferior— or whatever you've wished you weren't! Apply the teachings of the next four chapters first in your mind and then with actions that match your inner *I am.*

Here are a few examples:

- Addictions: Affirm, *I am sober; I am perfectly healthy.*
- Stuttering: Affirm, *I am in perfect command of my speech.*

- Poverty: Affirm, *I am prosperous.*

- Illness: Affirm, *I am well; I am perfect health.*

- Laziness: Affirm, *I am in possession of unlimited energy.*

- Seeking love: Affirm, *I am love, and I am in a loving relationship.*

- Intellectually weak: Affirm, *I am a genius.*

You might be thinking that this is all self-delusion, and just saying *I am* doesn't make it so. It's probably natural to feel skeptical if you believe that what your senses tell you is your only reality. The scriptures offer some words that may help you overcome your cynical viewpoint. The opening words in the book of John in the New Testament are: "In the beginning was the Word, and the Word was with God, and the Word was God" (John 1:1). Thirteen verses later, there is this phrase: "And the Word became flesh and dwelt among us" (John 1:14).

What do you suppose the phrase "and the Word was God" means? You are more than your sensory awareness. You are also your own spiritual divinity, which is impervious to those five senses. God proclaims in the same scriptures, as I noted in the previous chapter, "My name is I Am." Those two words are now in your imagination in such a way that they align perfectly with God. This is your beginning.

Steadfastly retain and repeat *I am,* and you will discover the reality of "and the Word became flesh and dwelt among us." Yes, the words *I am.* Calling upon this name and placing it in your imagination and living from this place literally joins you with the Source of power that allows you to become all that you've affirmed, as well as to create miracles. Begin by being willing to use these Divine words as the name of your highest self: God. That is the inauguration of the you that will live a wishes fulfilled life, as long as those wishes are in alignment with the Source of being, which is love—love for yourself and your magnificence, love for all of God's creations. You will observe with joyous bewilderment as the words *I am* become flesh and dwell in your life as a hardened fact.

Three Suggestions

— Commit yourself to your own magnificence. Every time you look into a mirror, remind yourself that what stares back at you is not an ever-changing body, but an invisibleness that is truly your highest self. Affirm: *I am love, I am God, I am worthy, I am infinite,* silently and out loud. Do this frequently so that it eventually becomes your inner mantra. This is not an ego exercise, it is an awakening to the incredible miracle that you are. This will help you abandon old patterns you've carried that have sullied your personal relationship to this universe and all of the inherent beauty and perfection it beholds.

— Fearlessly place *I ams* into your imagination. Recognize that previously, your false self, your ego, would never have allowed this expansion of your awareness. Ignore three-dimensional evidence that has defined your existence up until now. Enter into a higher fourth dimension that allows for the primary teaching of Jesus the Christ: "With God all things are possible." Your imagination is yours. You are free to place anything in there at your discretion. *I am talented, I am heroic, I am ecstatically happy, I am wealthy beyond words, I am content, I am God.* Be fearless, and let those ideals be your reality.

— Take this advice from *The "I AM" Discourses.* Decide what you want to do or become, and then, ignoring any and all interference, repeatedly say, "'I AM the Presence' doing it."[17] Treat this as your calling to love and adore your own mighty *I am* presence so that it always anchors and fortifies you. Every time you use the words *I am* with anything, you are also calling in the Divine power to do whatever you are proclaiming.

Implement these three suggestions and enter a dimension where there isn't a shred of doubt about your divinity and power.

SIX

THE THIRD
WISHES FULFILLED
FOUNDATION:

FEELING IT

*"That which you feel yourself to be you are, and you
are given that which you are. So assume the feeling that
would be yours were you already in possession of your wish,
and your wish must be realized. . . . So live in the feeling of
being the one you want to be and that you shall be."*[18]

—NEVILLE

I have a quotation on the wall near my bed that's from a re-
cording Neville made in 1944, which reads: "Make your future
dream a present fact, by assuming the feeling of the wish fulfilled." This is what I read and practice each night before I sleep.
These are the words that eventually prompted me to write this
book. They capture the essential message, not only of this chapter,
but this entire book. There is so much wisdom in this idea of
assuming the feeling of the wish fulfilled.

Until this point I've been explaining the importance of thoughts, thinking, self-concepts, and imagination. These are all invisible formulations that you enact. Your imagination and your concept of yourself are formless thoughts that you can change. Re-create your thoughts—making your imagination your own private inner territory—and ultimately you will act based on how you've used this amazing power that you possess. Furthermore, allowing your highest self to rule—thinking like God thinks—means all things are possible. Neville's books and lectures reveal something that makes his statement at the beginning of this chapter applicable to anyone seriously intent on mastering the art of manifestation. That *something* that Neville stresses throughout all his work is the importance of *feeling*.

"So live," he says, "in the feeling of being the one you want to be and that you shall be." This chapter invites you to realize the enormous implications this statement has for you. Become aware of the importance of feelings and their crucial role in advancing you from someone who merely *has* wishes to *experiencing* your wishes in your present life. So many people remain unaware of the importance of feeling that it's almost as if it were a secret ingredient to creating a wishes fulfilled life. The creative process begins with an idea, which the earlier chapters explored, including how to change your ideas about yourself and all that you are capable of achieving.

To summarize: the cycle of the creative process is first a thought, then a feeling, then a hardening into a physical object, or ultimately a new volitional act.

The Role of Feelings in Your Manifesting

To put it as plain and simple as I know how to make it: no assumption of the feeling of the wish fulfilled, no fulfillment of your wishes. In other words, it is absolutely imperative to learn how to assume, in your imagination, the feeling of already having and being what you desire. Your thoughts are without form. If we could find a location in space for these thoughts, they would be in your head—but your head has boundaries, and your thoughts do not have boundaries, so they could reside anywhere or nowhere.

You choose the thought that you prefer, from the trillions of thoughts that continuously flow through your mind on that never-ending conveyer belt. You can pick one that suits you, put it back, and take another at any time. Your imagination is the repository of thoughts that you opt to keep. Your *feelings,* on the other hand, are experienced in your body—the place where you do all of your living in this corporeal material world. Your feelings play more of a role in your life than you realize.

In order to learn something intellectually, you engage in the practice of mental discipline: studying, researching, memorizing facts, cogitating, participating in discussions, and seeking expert opinions. Ultimately you draw conclusions about what you've been analyzing. You know the facts and are confident you've mastered the subject through the thinking process.

Knowing something *spiritually* is a very different matter altogether. Here you can cogitate, ruminate, and analyze endlessly without accessing any more enlightened awareness of what you are studying. In order to know something spiritually, you must *experience* it, there is no other way—you cannot simply *think* your way to a new awareness. You must experience it, and the only vehicles you have for directly experiencing a new and higher vision for yourself are your feelings. *What does it feel like in your body?*

You may have placed a picture in your imagination of who you'd like to be, but if you can't assume the feeling of that wish fulfilled, you'll find it impossible to make your future dream a present fact. Yet you do have this wondrous power to take a thought that is in your imagination, live from that place in your daily life, and then experience in your body exactly how that feels and stay with this feeling. These words I am now channeling for you are among the most important you will read in this book, and perhaps in your entire lifetime. Your feelings are where you *live.* If you have been able to assume the feeling within your heart and genuinely feel the love that this activity brings to you, you will, as

Neville states, be in a place where your wish *must be realized*—such is the power of your feelings.

Years ago, while teaching at several major universities, I'd ask graduate students this question: "What do you respond to first—what you know, or how you feel?" I wanted them to determine which domain captured their primary attention. For instance, on the cognitive level—their analyzing ability, mathematical prowess, mastery of the rhyming scheme of an Elizabethan sonnet, or ability to memorize scientific formulas. On the feeling level—loneliness, sadness, fear, heartbreak, anxiety, love, ecstasy, joy, and so on. All reported that the feeling level was primary.

You most likely will agree that how you feel takes precedence over what you know—effect rules over cognition. Formal educational experiences, however, are almost exclusively devoted to the "what you know" aspect of your being. I'm suggesting that you assume an entirely new approach. I want you to get the full brunt of the message that the assumption of feeling of the wish fulfilled will bring home to you.

Here is Neville Goddard, speaking on this subject in 1944:

> Every feeling makes a subconscious impression and, unless it is counteracted by a more powerful feeling of an opposite nature, must be expressed. The dominant of two feelings is the one expressed. *I am healthy* is a stronger feeling than *I will be healthy.* To feel *I will be* is to confess *I am not; I am* is stronger than *I am not.* What you feel you are always dominates what you feel you would like to be; therefore, to be realized, the wish must be felt as a state that is rather than a state that is not.[19]

The words *I am strong* are simply cerebral abstractions. The *feeling* of *I am strong* is a sensation—and as Neville sums up: "Sensation precedes manifestation and is the foundation upon which all manifestation rests."[20] Here you are being encouraged to feel only the state you desire to realize. By literally feeling the reality of the state that you seek, which is firmly in your imagination, you have the means of creating miracles. "A change of feeling is a change of destiny."[21] Keep this beautiful tidbit from Neville omnipresent in your consciousness.

I have placed a thought in my imagination concerning the completion of this book and having it published and available to large numbers of people, including you. I have a picture of the completed book sitting in front of me, even though I am only halfway into the first draft. Yet these ideas and pictures are not the driving force that will allow my future dream to be the obvious present fact that it is.

I have assumed the feeling of the wish fulfilled, feeling the love in my body as I imagine millions of people learning these lessons that have so impacted my life. I look at the book jacket, I see the book as completed, and most important, I feel love in action. My subconscious mind has been programmed to act automatically on the desire I have placed in my imagination. But the actual fulfillment of that desire comes about because, and only because, I have assumed the feeling of the wish fulfilled within me right now, even though it appears that it has not yet materialized. To impress my subconscious mind with this desirable loving state I am currently experiencing, I assumed the feeling that would have been mine had I already realized my wish. This is really an exercise in discovering just how powerful a role our feeling state sensations play in the process of mastering the art of manifestation.

You are not engaging in an intellectual exercise, you are learning about your Divine spiritual nature and how God works as you. You can look at anything that you have declared in your imagination as *I am* and access the feeling of love in every cell of your body. You will in time impress your subconscious mind with all that it needs in order to match your desires with your reality.

Your Conscious and Subconscious Mind

Your conscious mind is private and it is always personal. It is the aspect of you that makes decisions, chooses this or that, and remains aware of what you do and how your decisions impact your volitional activities.

As a young boy I learned how to ice-skate by becoming conscious of every step along the way to be able to move and balance myself on a blade less than a centimeter across while on a surface of slick ice. My conscious mind kept correcting me, telling me to hold my arms out for balance, bend my knees in a certain way, turn the blades on my feet to the side to come to a halt, and so on. After spending time using my conscious mind to inform and direct my body to keep from falling, I became an accomplished hockey player and practically lived on the ice throughout my teenage years. That was my conscious mind at work.

Now fast-forward 40 years, and I'm staying at a home with a frozen-solid pond in the back acre during a cold winter in Massachusetts. I purchase a pair of ice skates, lace them up, and even though it has been almost four decades since I've been on the ice, off I go, skating as if I'd been doing so every day. All of the moves were there—I skated backward in circles and had the time of my life. The body I occupied didn't have one single cell remaining from the time when my *conscious mind* taught my *subconscious mind* how to skate all those decades earlier. In this example, my subconscious mind took over and allowed me to have an exhilarating day on the ice!

I'm sure you can recall times when your conscious mind generated ideas and impressed those ideas on your subconscious mind. This is how you learned to drive a car, do yoga exercises, cook a soufflé, and everything else that requires a multitude of complex maneuvers to do without the aid of your conscious mind. Your mind receives these ideas and ultimately gives form and expression to them. You have thoughts about trying something and then proceed to consciously practice, and you may not even realize that you are implanting the know-how in your subconscious mind. Your conscious mind is responsible for only 4 or 5 percent of all of your actions, including what you manifest.

Your subconscious mind—on autopilot once it has been imprinted by your conscious mind with its thoughts and ideas—

runs the show that is called *Your Life*. It accounts for some 96 percent or more of everything you do and everything you attract into your life. However, all things, including what you desire to manifest for yourself, evolve out of your thinking/conscious mind, and must then be impressed upon your subconscious mind. This is the cycle, and without this precise sequencing nothing will be made. Your feelings are deeply involved in this sequence.

The Role of Your Feelings in Fulfilling Your Wishes

Here's an observation from Neville regarding the importance of assuming the *feeling* of the wish fulfilled:

> Ideas are impressed on the subconscious through the medium of feeling. No idea can be impressed on the subconscious mind until it is felt, but once felt—be it good, bad or indifferent—it must be expressed. Feeling is the one and only medium through which ideas are conveyed to the subconscious.[22]

Your subconscious impressions are reflected in the conditions of your world. The strange and wonderful thing about your subconscious mind is that it always accepts as true what you feel to be true. The key words here are *feel to be true*. Your feelings allow your subconscious mind to spring into action. Earlier in this chapter I described intellectual understanding as tossing ideas around in your mind and drawing conclusions. Spiritual understanding differs in that it requires *experiencing* it. *The way to understand something spiritually is through experiencing it.* Your *feelings* are the tools you have for experiencing your subconscious mind and making it your material world reality.

Your feelings happen in your body, where you live and breathe. How you feel is your experience of life. These feelings flow from the thoughts you place in your imagination, and you are free to select any thought you desire. As I've reiterated throughout this book, when these thoughts are aligned with how your Source of being thinks, your feelings emanate as God-realized experiences within your body.

The utmost feeling that defines God, and your own highest self, is the feeling of love. "God is love, and he who abides in love abides in God, and God in him." Because your feelings, especially the feeling of love, are impressed on your subconscious mind, which is responsible for virtually everything that you do, experience, and manifest in your life—your mission is to get to that place of assuming the feeling of the wish fulfilled, even if the wish has yet to materialize in your physical reality.

Assuming the feeling of the wish fulfilled involves this fundamental awareness of how the subconscious mind works. Your subconscious mind is not personal; it is an expression of the one universal subconscious mind that we all use. This is a gnarly concept because your ego, where you spend the vast majority of your time, is so personal that you cannot grasp that we all share the same, the only, subconscious mind. As Neville states, "The subconscious is not selective; it is impersonal and no respecter of persons."[23] You want to keep tabs on what feelings you are associating with the wishes you have placed in your imagination, because whatever they are, you will see the universe aligning with them to provide experiences that match up with what you have impressed upon this universal subconscious mind.

Think thoughts like, *I am well, I am strong, I am prosperous,* and *I am employed;* place them into your imagination, and then assume the feeling of that wish fulfilled. If you can *experience the feeling* of love, joy, exhilaration, peace, and happiness in your body—even when your sensations are contradictory—your subconscious records the *feelings.* Neville is clear about this: "To impress the subconscious with the desirable state you must assume the feeling that would be yours had you already realized your wish."[24]

Feeling any state you wish to achieve is the experience that impresses it on the subconscious. Once again turning to Neville, he tells us, "The subconscious is the womb of creation. It receives the idea unto itself through the feelings of man. It never changes the idea received, but always gives it form."[25] *Always gives it form*—meaning that you must begin programming your sub-conscious mind, which will take over much like mine did when I laced up those ice skates without any prodding from my thinking or conscious mind in spite of a 40-year interval.

The subconscious mind accepts as true what you feel is true. Your feelings determine your reality because they're impressed on the subconscious. Consciously feeling hopeless, and entertaining this idea in your imagination with even more imaginative feelings of hopelessness, will impress on the subconscious mind the idea of failure. Consequently, you will be offered experiences by the one universal subconscious mind that will match what you've felt is true. Remember, the subconscious mind is impersonal and non-selective. It cannot make a distinction between what you feel as a result of your daily life experiences and what you feel as a result of what you have placed into your imagination as a future desire.

If you put the seed of failure into the subconscious and feed it with feeling that way, it will reproduce failure. If you plant the seed of disease into your subconscious mind by feeling this way in your body, it will augment disease for you. If you plant the seed of misery into your subconscious mind by feeling miserable, it will cultivate and produce misery for you. This is why it is so all-out crucial to begin *feeling* in your body what you would like to mani-fest into your life. You can get to the point where the magnetic-like power in your own field of energy is so joyfully loving that you can have a mere flash of imagining and feeling something power-ful and good, and with almost no passage of three-dimensional time it will appear in your life! Whatever you wish to manifest, associate a feeling of love with it and impress that feeling on the universal subconscious mind—and it will do the rest.

I am doing this as I contemplate the completion of this book in my imagination at this moment as I'm writing. I bathe this thought in pure love and feel the happiness that these words will bring to millions of people. I feel that loving sense of accomplish-ment in my entire being, inner and outer. The feeling I'm impress-ing on the subconscious mind is pure ecstatic love. God is love, and with God, all things are possible. I know the universal mind must act upon what has been impressed upon it. And *I am patient, and I am content.*

If you seek on the outside that which you are unwilling or unable to feel on the inside, you are seeking in vain. You attain that which you *are*—not simply what you want. Assume the feeling of the *wish fulfilled* and because you are experiencing it, that is what will manifest for you. The subconscious mind creates exactly what you believe in and can feel in your body.

Choosing to Feel Good

It is reported that Swami Muktananda asked each visitor entering his ashram if he knew the difference between feeling good and feeling God. If the devotee shook his head indicating he did not know, Muktananda would form a circle with his forefinger and thumb indicating zero—meaning there is zero difference between the two—God and good are one. "In the beginning God created the heavens and the earth" (Genesis 1:1). Thirty lines later, it is written in the Torah, "Then God saw everything that He had made, and indeed it was very good" (Genesis 1:31). God and all that He created is good. When you choose to feel good, you are choosing to feel what I described earlier as *your highest self*—the oneness that is called both good and God. Commit to making this your reality by repeating your intention to feel God-realized. Say to yourself, *I intend to feel good* or, as a synonym for God, *I intend to feel love.*

Don't dwell on your troubles, difficulties, or illnesses. The subconscious mind by its very nonselective nature accepts all your feelings associated with troubles as your request—and worst of all, proceeds to make them your experience in the world of your material reality. On the other hand, feeling love associated with what you have placed in your imagination triggers the subconscious mind to produce experiences that reflect its own Divine nature. Feel the feeling of love in your body directed at what you place in your imagination as an idea, and then you activate the subconscious mind.

The moment it receives a feeling impression, it takes action on working out the ways of its expression. I have been doing precisely this since I had a diagnosis of leukemia some two years ago. I place into my imagination an *I am* that says *I am strong; I am perfect health.* This is my imagination, and I can place any conscious thoughts in there that I choose, regardless of what my five senses might be saying to me. I live from this awareness of *I am strong; I am perfect health.* I talk to my body and remind it that I refuse to dwell on any *I am weak; I am sick* images.

The most important thing I do is choosing to feel good regardless of what the numbers on any medical screen might say. I meditate on *I am strong; I am perfect health; and I infuse my entire being, inner and outer, with a feeling of love and gratitude for this moment, this day, this body that has housed my invisible soul for these 71-plus years, and I assume the feeling of the wish fulfilled.* I have no thoughts of impending doom, only feelings of love for this miracle that I am. I treat my leukemia diagnosis as healing information being given to me rather than as a disease.

Can you imagine that God would build us in such a way that our cells would actually go to war with one another? War isn't even a concept that God is capable of implementing; war is a human concept—one that man has applied to his theories of how our body functions. What if all of these disease-model war theories are just as wrong in regard to our physical body as they are in resolving conflicts between people? What if what we call "illness" or "disease" is not that at all? What if we stopped looking at our health through scientific/medical theories and really looked at what our body is doing, and how it heals itself?

There are biological laws that your body abides by, and often what is labeled "disease" is actually your body's natural healing reflex. Perhaps it is a false belief that feeling unwell or having an abnormal blood count means you must fix it as quickly as possible. Must you search out a pill to fix everything? If you cut yourself, your body knows what to do—it forms a scab on its own.

The presence of a scab doesn't indicate that your body is out of balance and requires medical intervention. There's swelling, inflammation—and yes, some pain—but that isn't disease unless it becomes excessive. This way of recognizing your body's healing intelligence instead of treating it as a disease is equally true for psychological and emotional incidents.

Unexpected psychological events—such as the breakup of a marriage, a financial crisis, or the death of a loved one—create reactions in the brain that trigger physical responses in the body that are designed to assist the body in dealing with the conflict. The body continues to assist until the conflict is resolved, and then it goes into a healing phase to get back to its natural state of well-being. During this healing phase the body may utilize swelling, inflammation, fatigue, and an elevated white-blood-cell count as part of the healing process.

Leukemia, for instance, can actually be the healing phase of a severe psychological series of traumatizing events. This healing phase for leukemia first involves the expansion of blood vessels, lymph vessels, and a rise in leukocytes or leucoplasts; eventually, as the brain receives the healing message, blood cells of a good quality are produced, platelet counts return to normal, and energy levels rise. As I view it, my job is to heal any and all relationship conflicts and to feel completely valued, while eliminating and resolving any long-held conflicts and beliefs about myself. In other words, to feel good—that is, to feel God—and to offer unconditional love to everyone, including those who may have played a major part in any and all conflict dramas that once defined my life.

This is how I deal with a diagnosis of leukemia. I choose to feel good (God), to trust my body to use its inherent wisdom for healing, and to treat the diagnostic numbers in medical lab reports as what I'm supposed to be experiencing.

I go by *how I feel*, and the truth is, I am well, I am strong, and yes, I am God. I treat my body well, eat healthful and high-protein foods, rest, exercise, do yoga, and know that everything is in Divine hands and in Divine order. I view illness not as a failure on my part, but as the wonderful healing that it truly is, and I don't need pills, radiation, or invasive procedures.

The fact is that I feel good, and I am resolving any and all conflicts with massive doses of love (God is love, remember). This is what I choose to imprint on my subconscious mind, and the subconscious mind accepts as true that which I feel is true. Creation is the result of subconscious impressions, and by my feelings, I determine creation.

Impacting Your Subconscious Mind

As I close this section on the necessity of assuming the feeling of the wish fulfilled to facilitate your having an active role in manifesting a wishes fulfilled life, I offer you three reminders for how the subconscious mind works in collaboration with your feelings as a crucial component of this magnificent and mystifying process:

1. The subconscious mind responds to suggestions. You can reprogram your subconscious mind so that it goes on its accustomed role of autopilot with mental and feeling images from yourself. Talk to this automatically receptive component of yourself, telling it that you are unlimited, and that you believe all things are possible. Fill it with images of you being all that you dare to become. Go to a quiet place and feel in your body what it would feel like were those thoughts in your imagination your present reality.

2. The subconscious mind possesses the power to manifest physical reality from thought. Every object and circumstance in this world is representative of a mental thought. *All that now exists was once imagined*—such is the power of the subconscious mind. But in order to partake of this incredible powerhouse of creation that you are, you must be able and willing to experience within yourself—in your mind—that which you wish to manifest. Thoughts become things when you *feel* them, and are able to impress them upon the subconscious mind, which will then take over.

Here is how Neville describes this phenomenon: "This substance is consciousness. It is your imagination which forms this substance into concepts, which concepts are then manifested as circumstances, and physical objects. *Thus imagination made your world.*"[26] And then his take on the importance of feelings in programming the subconscious mind: "The reality of your assumption has its being in complete independence of objective fact and will clothe itself in flesh if you persist in the feeling of the wish fulfilled. When you know that assumptions, if persisted in, harden into facts, then events which seem to the uninitiated mere accidents will be understood by you to be the logical and inevitable *effects* of your assumption."[27]

3. Love is the feeling you must learn to assume. Subconscious mind is really a piece of the one mind, and you and I are living in that mind. This universal subconscious mind is the first cause, and the stuff from which all things are made. This *thingless* thing is really love. When you feel it, truly feel it within as your private inner awareness regarding what you would like to manifest, you gain the power of creation. Recall what Saint Francis of Assisi said in one line of his famous prayer: "Lord, make me an instrument of thy peace. Where there is hatred, let me sow love." You are asking in this prayer to have the feeling of the wish fulfilled.

When you experience anger, frustration, fear, doubt, worry, stress, and so on, ramp up your love and immerse those negative feelings in a container of pure love. Simply *choose* to feel good because every moment of offering love brings your little sliver of subconscious mind into harmony with the all-creating one universal subconscious mind that is defined as love.

I trust I've awakened within you the awareness that your feelings play a huge role in your becoming a God-realized manifesting being. Neville states this very clearly: "Denying the evidence of the senses and appropriating the feeling of the wish fulfilled is the way to the realization of your desire."[28] Apply his wisdom beginning now—it will serve you in ways that you may never have imagined in *common hours*. And remember that picturing the future without assuming the feeling of the wish fulfilled is nothing but futile daydreaming.

Three Suggestions

— Practice feeling a thought that you have inserted into your imagination. Remember that a feeling is what you feel in your body as you contemplate what it is you wish to manifest or who you would like to become. Close your eyes and experience what that feels like in your body. Work with sensations that are not only your experience of what you are imagining in your body but are triggers that assist you in moving from a thought to a hardened physical reality.

— Whatever feeling you are attempting to notice in your body regarding your wishes or desire, bathe it in *love*—the synonym for *God*. Imagine what you want. Imagine and feel that love as if you were now in possession of it. Continue doing this using love, until your desire actually belongs to you. During this process remind yourself that the more love (God) you offer, the sooner desire becomes reality. Look into your mirror fearlessly, saying, *I not only love you—I am love.*

— Acquaint yourself with the subconscious mind. Your piece of subconscious mind acts on what you program into it so that it becomes your automatic mind acting habitually. Decide on a habit that you would like to be automatic—being generous, for example. Tell yourself, *I am a generous person.* Give something away in a spirit of generosity, even if it's only a small coin or a word of encouragement.

The more thoughts and actions you practice around your new *I am,* the more the subconscious mind will react in kind until eventually it will act in generous ways out of a new habit that you've created. You have the power to impress upon the subconscious mind any *I am* of your choosing.

THE FOURTH WISHES FULFILLED FOUNDATION:

YOUR ATTENTION PLEASE

"Your imagination is able to do all that you ask
in proportion to the degree of your attention."[29]

— NEVILLE

As you work at mastering this art of manifestation, you are going to receive a great deal of information, advice, and probably pressure concerning the ideas and objectives you have placed into your imagination. As you successfully ramp up your awareness of your imagination, you will begin to make this private inner world a more active component of your everyday living. Trusting that what you are thinking is more than just a mental exercise, you will begin living from this new place within you. This inner invisible world of yours will be the source of your new reality.

Through determination and unabated intention, you can begin the process of assuming the feeling of the wish fulfilled, imagining it, living from it in your mind, and feeling it in your body. If you are unwilling to place your attention on a salubrious application of all of these new elements, all of your efforts will assuredly be in vain. The key word here is *attention.*

When you decide and begin to use the information presented here to live a wishes fulfilled life, you are going to encounter a great deal of notice in a variety of forms. Friends and associates will offer uninvited opinions concerning this new you and what you're attempting to manifest. Your immediate family may try to dissuade you from making any changes that they think might cause them to feel inadequate or uncomfortable. You'll be presented with *scientifically verifiable* facts to deter you from believing in your unlimited self. Strangers will relate stories about someone who died attempting to do what you are thinking about. Stories of the absurdity of your desires being manifested will be sent to you in the hope that you will realize that you are not a Divine being. You might be threatened with punishment from God, or Jesus, or the devil, or some spiritual deity who's angered and going to put a curse on you for offending their sensibilities.

As you engage in the process of living from your highest self, trusting in your own God-realized strengths and becoming more peaceful and content, all the while feeling the love you are choosing to align with—your new ideas about who you are and what you can accomplish and become will be noticed positively and negatively. You may have to convince yourself to be steadfast in the attention that you place on the wishes you are going to fulfill. Never let your attentiveness to what you are in the process of manifesting be sidetracked by external pressures of any kind. As Neville reminds you, "All progress, all fulfillment of desire, depend upon the control and concentration of your attention."[30]

One of the things I love about my new iPad that was given to me by my children is the feature that is called TRASH. What a concept! I'd like you to implement this technology in all areas of your life. When you receive information or a request that runs counter to the *I ams* that you have placed in your imagination, simply push that TRASH button in your mind, and watch it sail over to the left side of your "screen" . . . and then mentally touch the DELETE button. This is how you keep your attention focused on what you are manifesting into your life.

You are in the flow of a new consciousness that has no limitations. You are thinking, feeling, and acting as a Divine being, a part of the universal one mind that knows that *all things are possible.* Yet you live in a world where this stance is often considered insane and outright preposterous. You have to choose what kind of attention you give to the feedback you will receive. Essentially, there are two modes of attention that you can choose from—objective and subjective. Objective attention is the most common —abandon it in favor of subjective attention.

Objective and Subjective Attention: It's Always Your Choice

You employ *objective attention* when you monitor external input such as information and attitudes that originate outside of you. This is an important aspect of functioning in your life. However, you need to consciously bring into your awareness your ability to select and switch between objective and subjective attention. With awareness and practice you will discover that by employing subjective attention first, you almost magically are released from an addiction to external impressions. It is your choice—and the rewards are exponential! *Do not give attention to what others do or fail to do; give attention to what you do or fail to do,* is sage advice.

Whatever wish you have placed into your imagination will engender stimulus responses. Those responses that come to you from the external world, while often valuable as feedback, are things that you are going to work at ignoring if they in any way represent an obstacle to the fulfillment of your dream. Here is what Neville has to say concerning these two disparate approaches to how you should place your own attention: "There is an enormous difference between attention directed objectively and attention directed subjectively, *and the capacity to change your future depends on the latter.*"[31] Becoming a wishes fulfilled person involves learning to strategically employ your subjective attention.

Whatever you are placing in your imagination and feeling is present will become a part of your daily life, suddenly appearing in many of your conversations and activities. Television, movies, Internet tidbits, and news reports on the same subject will make their way to your consciousness. Contradictory information may appear out of nowhere. There will be friends and strangers who want to express their opinions and share their stories about someone who attempted to do what you are working on. This is when having learned to differentiate between subjective or objective attention and practicing choosing one or both becomes critically important to your success. Start with *subjective attention.*

Put your subjective attention on the *I am* that you have firmly planted in your imagination, and refuse to allow any external data to interfere with directing your loving attention on the subjective *I am.* Attend first to the feeling within you by giving it your wholehearted attention rather than reacting toward the external person or influence. Redirect your attention with trust, love, and kindness from outside to inside. This is called subjective attention. This is the way that you operate whenever the subject matter of the future you and all that you are manifesting arises in your field of awareness.

The objectified opinions and information that enter your field of awareness are excellent reminders to redirect your attention to love for, and belief in, your ability to manifest wishes fulfilled. Once again, Neville reminds you that "When you are able to control the movements of your attention in the subjective world, you can modify or alter your life as you please. But this control cannot be achieved if you allow your attention to be attracted constantly from without."[32]

If you have read my books and listened to my lectures over the years, you have heard me cite Carlos Castaneda's work on many occasions. He was a great teacher for me, often telling powerful

stories about the exalted world of impeccability, where one transcends ordinary levels of awareness. I've become friendly with his
wife, who recently celebrated her 90th birthday. She told me she'd
written a four-line poem that expressed Carlos's ideas as well as
those of Neville, whose many lectures she had attended as a young
woman. I asked her to send it to me so that I could include it in
this section on using your attention to create the objectified life
you desire.

I place it here for you to consider:

> *When you think, choose carefully*
> *The thoughts of things you'd like to be . . .*
> *Thoughts entertained in the minds of men*
> *Become Tomorrow's objectified whims.*

> — MARGARET RUNYAN CASTANEDA

As you read and reread Margaret's words, note that everything
that you materialize into this objectified physical reality is really nothing more than a whim, but in order to experience it as
your reality—though it is but an illusion, since all is continuously
changing—it must come from the *subjective* thoughts that you,
and only you, must choose very carefully.

I am asking you here to ignore every bit of information that's
directed at you if it in any way contradicts the *I am* you've placed
in your imagination. This is particularly relevant when it comes to
the data you receive from your own senses. Yes, I am saying that
even your own eyes and ears are objective inputs. An x-ray that
shows you have a tumor that you can feel with your fingers contradicts the *I am* in your imagination that says, *I am perfect health.*
You want to decide to live *from* the end you're wishing for—not
toward an end that others have decided for you. Thus, you must
discard what your senses tell you, and stay with your subjective
attention, persistently and adamantly proclaiming, *I am perfect
health.* Your subjective attention is unrelated to what you have
conditioned your subconscious mind to believe to be your reality

as indicated by what your five senses so convincingly tell you. You are the *I am that I am,* and "that" is your tumor-free existence.

Redirect your attention *away* from debates aimed at disputing or convincing an external attitude and toward *placing your attention on the feeling* of the wish fulfilled. The outcome depends on your inner attitude—your subjective attention. You might consider being like a pit bull—teeth firmly planted on a rubber bone. You must attach yourself spiritually to what you have placed in your imagination as a future fact, and never allow anyone, anything, any circumstance, no matter how persuasive their case, to alter what you know to be your destiny. Every single item that brings up the subject of what you are in the process of creating for yourself must immediately trigger in you a response of putting all of your mental, emotional, and physical attention on the *I am* that you have placed in your imagination. This is where using that wonderful TRASH button will be immensely useful to you.

You can do everything right in the first three foundations of a wishes fulfilled life, but if you allow your attention to be diverted by an outer stimulus and abandon even for a moment the *I am* in your imagination, you will delete the entire project. Develop a healthy attitude toward your highest self, and all that it beckons you to be, by redirecting a habit of being influenced by outer objective factors to trusting your ability to choose subjective attention, and focusing on inner rather than outer directives.

Abraham Maslow spent a good part of his adult life researching and writing about the idea of self-actualization. He described the small percentage of people he called "self-actualizing" as living at the extraordinary level of consciousness that I mentioned in the opening pages of this book. I vividly recall Dr. Maslow's assertion that one of the highest qualities these self-actualizers possess is the inclination to be *independent of the good opinion of others.* Dr. Maslow presented his data and explained it brilliantly to the academic community.

I'm deeply attracted to this idea of living extraordinarily—independent of the good opinion of others—stressing it in many of the books and recordings I've produced, starting in 1971.

Dr. Maslow passed away on June 8, 1970, the same day I received my doctorate degree—I've often felt that in some mystical way, he was passing the baton to me.

Choosing to be aware of your attention and managing to select subjective attentiveness harmonizes with one of Dr. Maslow's most significant attributes of living a self-actualized life: trusting yourself. When you trust yourself to decide what is to be your destiny, you don't allow externals to discourage or influence you. What you place your attention on is your burning desire and intense yearning combined with an intention to make that your reality. You never allow outer circumstances to deflect you from your desires. This inner picture in your imagination is undisturbed by opinions or provocations that originate outside of yourself.

Subjective attention means that you and only you are the subject that impacts the burning desires in your imagination. Remember, these ideas in your imagination are simply thoughts that are being treated by you as present facts. You are living and feeling as if your future dream is a present fact. Allowing a research report, news story, contrary opinion, contradictory incident, pronouncement by a government agency, new law, or anything else to take your attention away from the wishes in your imagination dismantles and destroys your desired outcome.

You must have faith, and faith is attained through complete trust and confidence in the power of the one universal mind, which you are inextricably a piece of. It is the God-realized you that placed those thoughts and feelings into your mind and your body. You are the subject here, and therefore you must trust in your subjective attention and not allow external objective factors to hold sway over how you use your attention.

One of the reasons I'm able to write about the hidden power of manifestation buried deep within each of us is that during childhood I unconsciously practiced these ideas while in foster homes—and they simply became a part of who I am. Throughout my life I've been labeled "stubborn," "obsessive," "headstrong," and "unyielding" when it comes to what I have in my imagination and seeing it become my physical reality.

In order to assume the feeling of the wish fulfilled, you must be able to feel it in your body long before your senses are aware of it. This requires tenacity on your part and an unwillingness to allow your imagination, where all things are created, to be objectified by anything external to yourself. When you are adamant about not letting your attention be directed by outer influences, you are in the process of developing a habit that works *for,* rather than *against,* you. Your inner pictures and the corresponding feelings that are connected to your vision belong only to you, and you begin to treat this inner world of thoughts and feelings as sacred territory. You make the shift from *believing* to *knowing,* and what you absolutely know is not tinged with doubt. As William Shakespeare put it, "Our doubts are traitors." Anyone or anything trying to diminish your inner feelings with doubt is a traitor to be banished.

With a recent diagnosis of leukemia I've done precisely what I'm writing about, in the same way that I have for my entire life, concerning my own fate and my own well-being. What I know for certain is that there's an emotional component to every illness. As I indicated earlier, I view my elevated white-blood-cell count as part of my body employing its God-realized intelligence to heal whatever damage I've caused by participating in psychologically traumatic activities, particularly in my relationships with loved ones.

So rather than cursing my body's innate wisdom, I am in a profound state of gratitude for all that has come my way, including these elevated blood-cell counts. The more I assume the feeling of my *I am well; I am strong* assertions in my imagination, the more the universe seems to send me the right information and the right people to assist me in living a wishes fulfilled life. One particular incident stands out.

The day that I received the diagnosis of chronic lymphocytic leukemia, I "coincidentally" met Pam McDonald, who had flown to Maui to see if I would be willing to collaborate with her in her integrative-medicine practice. She'd been using my previously published materials with great success, helping her patients heal from a wide variety of diseases and illnesses—such as obesity, heart disease, diabetes, Alzheimer's, and many cancers and addictions that are so widespread they threaten our collective physical well-being.

Pam is a nurse-practitioner in Northern California. When I told her of the diagnosis I'd received that very morning, she responded, "Now I know why I was sent here—not to enlist your aid in my practice, but to serve you." On the very day I received my diagnosis, Pam appeared in my life, committed to being a primary health-care provider for me.

Pam explained that correcting unhealthy nutritional habits can realign us with the specific genetic blueprint that we are born with. Amazing healing takes place with corrective genetic alignment, which treats diseases that are associated with inflammatory diets and the way our body processes fats and cholesterol. When we begin to eat consciously, in harmony with our desire to feel good and be well, the markers for these supposedly incurable diseases begin to return to normal.

Subsequently, she (all at her own expense) tested my blood for my APO E gene and even flew to Southern California while I was at the Chopra Center for Wellbeing visiting Deepak. Step-by-step, she explained an easy-to-adopt nutritional plan that I've followed to a point where two of the eight markers for chronic lymphocytic leukemia (CLL) have headed back to normal. Pam McDonald was an angel sent to me in my time of need. She has toured with me and spoken to thousands of people at my public lectures.

Pam has become a personal health-care practitioner, and has now helped me and many thousands of others to improve their health. She's written a powerful book, titled *The Perfect Gene Diet*, explaining all this in professional detail. I'm proud to have written the Foreword, testifying to the beneficial results that are waiting for you if you become conscious of your eating habits and your food intake so that it aligns with the genetic profile you've inherited. Make a commitment to your own highest state of physical well-being by becoming aware that everything you eat impacts your ability to facilitate the healing that your body craves.

I decided from day one to assume the feeling of my wish fulfilled for a healthy body. The truth is, I feel good, I am well, I am strong, and I categorically refuse to entertain any other input that conflicts with my *I ams*. I know that when I stay in this place, aligned with my highest self and the universal one mind responsible for all of creation, almost magically—in what Carl Jung called "synchronicity"—things begin to happen that can't happen when one is thinking and feeling from a non-well-being state. Pam showing up that day *coincidentally* impacted my health, my outlook, my well-being, and yes, my healing. Her presence in my life is now affecting huge numbers of people all over the world, and absolutely could usher in a new era of well-being for the entire planet.

It isn't a stretch for me to say that by assuming the feeling of a wish fulfilled, and using your subjective attention to deflect any and all naysayers, you and many more like you can literally end some of the epidemics that threaten the entire population of the world. It's that big!

The Movement of Your Attention and Your I Ams

You have many ideas concerning the person you'd like to be, as well as what you'd like to manifest in your life. You've placed those ideas into your imagination, and you're willing to live *from* rather than *toward* those ends. You recognize your opportunities to assume the feeling in your body of those wishes fulfilled—though they're currently in your mind and not yet in your everyday material world. You now need to know what to do when the subject matter of your wishes comes up in any way—be it from other people, external events, or even you tossing the matter over and over in your mind. What you do or do not do will make all the difference in the manifestation of your ideals.

What you do is not necessarily what action you take, but rather where you choose to place your mental attention. What you do with what is in your mind is what I mean by your *attention*. So do not let *your attention* be affected by anything or anyone, regardless of the tone or feedback being positive or negative, around where you are in the process of manifesting. Your *I ams* planted firmly in your inner mental sanctum will provide you with the strength and the power to keep your attention *subjectively* focused.

What follows are ways to consider the significance of making the shift from objective to subjective in the application of your personal attention.

Your Intention Is to Experience the Healing of Your Body

When referring to her near death experience (NDE), Anita Moorjani (introduced earlier in this book) said, "I was shown how illnesses start on an energetic level before they become physical. If I chose to go into life, the cancer would be gone from my energy, and my physical body would catch up very quickly. I then understood that when people have medical treatments for illnesses, it rids the illness only from their body but not from their energy, so the illness returns. I realized if I went back, it would be with a very healthy energy. Then the physical body would catch up to the energetic conditions very quickly and permanently." Can you be open to the idea that Anita learned, while in her near-death state, that all illness starts at an energetic level?

You don't have to know what the state of your energetic predisposition for some illness might be—all you need to do is align your subconscious mind with the conscious suggestion that you have an energy body, and if you can heal the *energy* that presupposed your illness, then you can quickly and permanently heal your physical body. You might say that this is grandiosity, and it just offers false hope to those who are incurably ill.

I always loved the words of Michelangelo regarding this subject: "The greater danger is not that our hopes are too high and we fail to reach them, it's that they are too low, and we do." Hopes are thoughts in your imagination that you can change into present-day facts. You do so by assuming the feeling of the wish fulfilled and choosing to use your new *I ams* as facts that you *feel* and give subjective attention to.

When you experience any kind of maladjustment in your body, you are offered a great deal of *objective* information to consider. "A friend of mine died from what you have," "Here's some published research describing what you have as incurable," "Trust modern medicine rather than these airy-fairy ideas," "One-third of the population successfully deals with the same condition with medication while your malady gets worse because you refuse medication"—these and thousands like them are objective offerings. You need to remain alert to your *subjective attention* by going to the *I am* that you have placed in your imagination and assume the feeling in your body of that wish already fulfilled.

Here's an offering from *The "I AM" Discourses* by Saint Germain: "A remarkable Statement that would be enormously helpful to the students would be to say: '"I AM" the Miracle-Working Presence in everything I require to have done.'"[33] This is subjective attention at work in you. You are the *I am* presence, if you trust in your highest self. And your highest self fearlessly proclaims *I am God*.

Begin to trust in the *I am* presence—it is your very essence as a spiritual being having a temporary human experience. Persistently place your fulfilled wishes in your subconscious mind with sentences like, *I am the almighty governing presence of my life and my world,* and *I am the health, well-being, and harmony, self-sustained, which carries me through everything that confronts me.* Trust in your inner guidance and your Divine connection to the creator of worlds, rather than giving so much credence to whatever objectified information appears in your daily life that is an assault on your spiritual nature.

Your Intention Is to Attract Prosperity and Abundance into Your Life

To attract appropriate and healthy prosperity or abundance into your life, you need to place all of your attention on what that *feels* like. You need to be able to *feel* what that is like even before it materializes to your satisfaction. By feeling those pleasant sensations in your body, you reprogram your segment of subconscious mind to harmonize with the infinitely prosperous universal subconscious mind where all manifestation originates. Your ability to wholeheartedly align with this energetic field means that you simply never again produce thoughts like, *I hope someday to become prosperous.*

Spend some time seriously considering the implications in this passage from Neville's *The Power of Awareness:* "'I will be' is a confession that *'I am not.'* The Father's will is *always* 'I AM.' Until you realize that YOU are the Father (there is only one I AM, and your infinite self is that I AM), your will is always *'I will be.'*"[34]

Chapter Three in this book, on your highest self, introduced you to the impossibility for the Source of all to say, "I will be," because to do so is to say, "I am not." How could God say, "I am not"? *Wanting* to attract more prosperity into your life is equivalent to sending the message of *I am not.* As long as this is your conscious thought, you are unwittingly programming your subconscious mind to offer you experiences that match your feeling. *I am not* projects a state of lack. There will be an avalanche of objective thoughts and ideas thrown at you regarding the intention you have of experiencing a life of prosperity. I know this personally because I've heard it all my life.

As a student of human nature, I long ago came to the conclusion that most people do not know how to make money or attract abundance. It's a rare person indeed who is the exception to this observation, although I am certain that you—yes, you—are in the process of leaving that mind-set behind. Many people feel that their life isn't fulfilled because they do not trust their own highest self. Quite likely this is so because they didn't discover earlier in life that they even have a higher or highest self. When a person knows that he or she is God and has awareness of his or her own divinity, it is impossible to say, "I will be." Why? Because "I will be" means "I am not."

Your subjective attention is how you choose to *think,* and especially *feel,* about what you've placed in your imagination. The words that Srimati Kashi Moni, the "sacred mother," spoke to Paramahansa Yogananda in his book *Autobiography of a Yogi* have stayed with me my entire adult life: "Seek divine wealth, not the paltry tinsel of earth. After acquiring inward treasure, you will find that outward supply is always forthcoming."

Your *inward treasure* is your feeling of living in a world of unlimited abundance. Refuse to allow any external data to deflect you from what you have placed in your imagination. Always live from your subjective feelings of *I am prosperous; I am wealthy; I am content.* With your imagination, you will then program your subconscious mind to align with experiences that match what you feel in your body.

As a young boy living in a foster home, I always knew that I could attract spending money into my world, even though most of the children around me seemed only to know scarcity and that's what they always seemed to attract. As a young man I knew inwardly that money would chase me if I acted on my feelings. As Paramahansa Yogananda's sacred mother's advice relates, I seemed to seek the Divine wealth of inner feelings and knew that the outward supply would find me.

I was told by objectified attention that being a schoolteacher ensured that I'd never have wealth because it's a low-paying profession, but I expunged such silliness from my inner world. The same was true for my writing, my lecturing, and all of my other professional activities. I feel prosperous, and I know that I will continue to act on my inner experiences of abundance—and that universal mind will also offer me the right people, events, and circumstances guiding me on this spiritual path of extraordinary higher awareness.

My story concerning the manifestation of abundance throughout my life is never allowing anyone, no matter how persuasive, to infiltrate my imagination, which feels prosperous and able to attract unlimited abundance. By holding this inner view as sacrosanct, and never allowing anything to besmirch this inner knowing, I acted in ways that produced prosperity—but the universe always seems to send me the assistance I require to make my future dreams a present fact.

Here is Saint Germain in *The "I AM" Discourses* on the power you possess as a result of your very beingness: "The moment you say 'I AM,' you set in motion this Power that has inherent within It all these faculties. It has all substance, and must take on whatsoever form the attention of the mind is fixed upon. The 'I AM' is the Fathomless Mind of God."[35] Use this fathomless mind of yours to place your attention always on what is aligned with your Source of being—the unlimited abundance that is the highest good for all concerned.

Your Intention Is to Live a Life of Happiness

Happiness isn't some *thing* in the material world that can be acquired and stored and used when needed or wanted. If it were, I'd give you a lifetime supply that would guarantee a happy life. No—happiness is an attitude that comes from within you. It's accessible when you place in your imagination an *I am* statement that reflects your attunement with the simple truth that happiness is indeed an inside job. Happiness is an inner belief that you bring to everyone and everything you undertake, rather than expecting your happiness to come to you from others or from your accomplishments and acquisitions. *There is no way to happiness, happiness is the way.*

State your intention to live a happy, contented life; place it squarely in the most prominent place within your imagination, and live from that place as if it were your reality. When circumstances and/or your five senses try to influence you that you're wrong, gently and with loving confidence let the fearful or naysaying thoughts drift by like passing clouds as you focus on your nourishing imagination, which cannot be altered without your agreement. Neville speaks without hesitation on this matter: "The promise is definite that if you are shameless in your impudence in assuming that you *already have* that which your senses deny, it shall be given unto you—*your desire shall be attained.*"[36]

Don't be dismayed when you encounter people and circumstances that attempt to convince you the *I am happy* assertion that you've placed in your imagination is absurd. Don't let these objective attempts influence you to assume the feeling of a wish for *unhappiness* to be fulfilled! Persist in stating your inner mantras of *I am happy* and *I am content* while assuming the feeling in your body of this already fulfilled—or as Neville stated, be "shameless in your impudence" in assuming the feeling of happy contentment.

This means that you permit only your personal subjective attention to align with your inner *I am* declaration. Your subconscious mind understands who you intend to be, and you will naturally discontinue inviting or entertaining any form of "I have a right to be miserable," "How could I ever be happy with the circumstances that define my life?" "My parent, spouse, sister [any external relationship] make me unhappy," and so on. How is it ever possible for God to say, "I am miserable" or "I am unhappy"? Remember, you have a highest self, and it is one with God.

Here is Saint Germain speaking on this subject in a transmission received on November 24, 1932:

> I would suggest that those who have been having unpleasant experiences would consciously withdraw from those conditions all power they have been giving them, mostly unknowingly. When it is necessary to discuss some condition to understand it, immediately follow by withdrawing any power that has been given it, and then know, "'I AM' the Harmonious Presence, ever pervading whatever the condition may be."
>
> When I say: "'I AM' the Governing Presence,'" "I AM" fully, consciously aware that I have set in motion the Full Power and Intelligence of God producing the desired conditions, and that they are thus Self-sustained.[37]

I urge you to read and sustain this message regarding your own happiness. Be dedicated to your own subjective attention—always reminding it and yourself that *I am the harmonious and governing presence.* You will activate the power of God because you are at one with your all-creating Source.

Whether it's your health, wealth, happiness, or any other element of your entire life experience, it is essential to keep in mind the importance of the movement of your attention. You must be obstinate and persistent in not allowing the viewpoints or information of others to alter your inner world. You know what you wish to become and what you would like to manifest for yourself. Now keep your imagination so aligned and feel it in your body. Using your subjective attention will produce the desired conditions.

Three Suggestions

— Become conscious of objective efforts designed to persuade you to abandon the ideas and ideals you have tucked away in your imagination. As your awareness intensifies, practice a subjective alternative to those objective efforts. Whenever your attention is drawn to negating what you are in the process of manifesting, close your eyes, sit quietly for a moment, and repeat your *I am* to yourself over and over until you feel it reverberating within your body. Be on guard—ready and willing to dismiss any objectified information that conflicts with your inner vision. The more you practice this, the less your old mind viruses will impact you. Soon there will be a new embedded trust in your ability to manifest the life you desire.

— Use what I call the superglue method for placing intentions into your imagination: Imagine you have a substance that's so strong it can't weaken or break. This is the stuff you dab on your *I am* as it is placed in your private inner domain. It's equivalent to saying, "Nothing external to myself has the power to remove what I place on my inner screen." When you say, "I am healthy,"

"I am prosperous," "I am happy," or any other *I am,* you are using the name of God, which is inviolable as far as you're concerned. This is a spiritual decision on your part to become the ideal that you know deep within you is your calling. The superglue metaphor will remind you to use only your subjective attention when your wishes fulfilled intentions are visible to others.

— Inner intentions are a private matter between you and your Source of being. Inviting others to support or consider your intentions is an invitation to their objective attention. Responses are often designed to convince you that your intention is an impossible dream. You'll be in the position of defending (or at the very least, explaining) yourself. This is an invitation to ego, who will leap at this opportunity to shift your inner intentions and dispute the external, supposedly logical or scientific facts that are coming your way.

Manifestation is a spiritual exercise. Thus, it defies logic, facts, past experiences, scientific evidence, and all sorts of objective opinions. Keep it a private matter in the spirit of Neville: "Therefore, when you know what you want, you must deliberately focus your attention on the feeling of your wish fulfilled until that feeling fills the mind and crowds all other ideas out of consciousness."[38]

Keep your intentions private—avoiding the necessity of deflecting well-meaning opinions from external forces.

I end this chapter with the words of Saint Paul in his letters to the Philippians. This is one of my favorite verses in the New Testament:

*"I am not saying this because I am in need, for
I have learned to be content whatever the circumstances"
(Philippians 4:11).*

This is the ultimate use of subjective attention.

THE FIFTH
WISHES FULFILLED
FOUNDATION:
NOW I LAY ME DOWN TO SLEEP

*"In a dream, in a vision of the night, when deep sleep
falls upon men, while slumbering on their beds, then
He opens the ears of men, and seals their instruction."*

— JOB 33:15-16

It is in sleep that you enter the world of your subconscious
mind, and it is here that you will be making your impression and
receiving your instructions, as indicated in this biblical quote
from the book of Job. I would like you to think about the nature
of your subconscious mind, which has been programmed by your
conscious mind to act habitually; that is, *without thinking* about
what you are doing or not doing. You, no doubt, will have recol-
lections like the one I just had.

I recall being 15 years old, learning to drive a standard-shift car. I was using my conscious mind to practice a seemingly endless list of maneuvers with a thought process that went something like this: *I have a car here with three foot pedals, and I only have two feet to work with. I must push my left foot down on the clutch pedal, and with my right foot on the accelerator pedal, slowly—and I mean very slowly—let the clutch pedal out while simultaneously pushing down on the accelerator pedal with the same amount of pressure with my right foot as the pressure I'm releasing with my left foot on the clutch pedal. Too much gas, or not enough clutch, and the car will stall . . . and then there's that third pedal for braking, which I have no idea how to use, as the car keeps lurching forward. Which foot? How much pressure?*

On and on went my conscious mind, trying to master this seemingly impossible task of learning to drive without jerking the car and stalling the engine. Then came the time when I was on a steep incline of a hill waiting for a red light to turn green—while I sat there with one foot on the clutch, one foot on the brake to keep the car from rolling backward down the hill into the car behind me, and no feet left over for the all-important gas pedal to move forward!

My point is that my conscious mind was sending impressions and instructions to my subconscious mind until ultimately I no longer needed my conscious mind to drive a standard-shift car. It all became automatic, and my habitual subconscious mind took over and did it all for me. This subconscious mind of mine didn't care how I was feeling, how much time had passed since I'd previously driven, what I believed, what others said about the difficulty of driving a standard-shift car—all it did was react to the programming I had offered it, and then took over the act of driving smoothly and effortlessly without my ever having to think about it again.

Thirty years passed, and I took my family to Italy for a two-week tour. When we rented a car in Milan, the only one available was a Fiat with a clutch, brake, and accelerator pedal. I hadn't driven a standard-shift car in three decades, yet my subconscious mind knew precisely what to do and took over the driving for our entire time in Italy. Much like the ice-skating story I wrote about earlier, that habitual mind of mine had been sufficiently trained and needed no further reminders in order to take on the present-day task. The subconscious mind is forever imprinted once it has been sufficiently programmed and received its instruction—it simply takes over, and the conscious mind is seldom needed.

Your subconscious mind handles about 96 percent of all that you undertake in your life. It is as if you are placed on automatic pilot for almost everything that you do each and every day of your life. The examples of learning to drive a standard-shift car and ice-skating bring it home clearly in the dimension of your physical body. You train it to act automatically once the conscious mind is no longer needed. This same programming functions successfully in every area of your life, including your ability to manifest a wishes fulfilled life.

Preparing for Sleep and Your Subconscious Mind

Sleep is the time when your conscious mind leaves the world of your five senses and joins in with your subconscious mind. Your subconscious habitual mind is uninterested in changing your conscious beliefs or feelings. It simply responds to what has been programmed into it. Neville reminds us that "The unconsciousness of sleep is the normal state of the subconscious."[39] You spend one-third or more of your entire time here in this incarnation in this normal state of the subconscious mind. This is where you receive instructions for how the other two-thirds of your life can unfold. Here is where you receive instructions for running your life smoothly, effortlessly, and miraculously.

It's similar to the mode of consciously learning to drive a stick shift, master the computer, knit a sweater, swim, dance, hit a golf ball, and all the other multitude of activities you perform in your waking moments, usually without having to think about how to do them. Including what you are doing right here in this moment: reading a book!

The most significant thing that I want you to capture and apply from this chapter is not so much what you do while you are dreaming and sleeping, but how you prepare yourself for entering into your unconscious state of sleep.

Sleep is the natural state for your subconscious mind, which rules about 96 percent of your waking life. The last five minutes of your day before you enter into your sleep state are the most important five minutes of your day if you are going to begin living a wishes fulfilled life. In this brief portion of your day, you are going to tell your subconscious mind how you feel and what wishes God (the universal one subconscious mind) is to fulfill upon awakening from your deep slumber. This five-minute segment of time in your bed, about to enter into your subconscious and marinate for the next eight hours or so, is the most crucial segment of your entire 24-hour day.

You can use this time in one of two ways. Let me explain them both to you, and then you can decide which one you choose to adopt for yourself, keeping in mind that what you impress upon your subconscious mind is what the universal one subconscious mind will offer you in your waking hours. Your subconscious mind is indifferent to what you want or what is best for you. It cannot make a distinction between what you are feeling as a result of all that happens to you throughout your waking hours, or what you feel as a result of what you are imagining for yourself as having already transpired while you are in bed preparing to doze off to sleep.

1. Choosing to Review the Day's Frustrations and Disappointments

As you lie in bed, you can use this time prior to entering your subconscious mind to review everything that transpired throughout the day that caused you to feel unhappy, dejected, frustrated, angry, and so on. You can think sad thoughts about all of the people who disappointed you, and review in your imagination (via inner dialogue with yourself) how unhappy all of that made you. You can spend these critical moments worrying about all of the things that didn't work out the way you wanted them to, and projecting onto your subconscious mind evidence for things continuing to transpire in the same way that they always have. You can go over the arguments you had with others, and conclude that those people really do make you unhappy. You can use your mind to relive how fearful you are that things are not going to improve. You can even predict that a great calamity is about to befall you and your family, and there is nothing to be done to stave it off.

You can picture in your mind the worst possible outcome concerning your own health or the health of a loved one. You can imagine yourself filing for bankruptcy, or not getting the job you desire, or a natural disaster striking you, or you feeling even sicker when you awaken. The potential disasters that you can entertain with your thoughts as you prepare to go to sleep could fill the next 100 pages.

Whatever you opt for—such as these examples of thoughts that make you feel bad—is a *choice* to send those messages to your subconscious just as you are about to go to sleep. In effect, you are imprinting your subconscious with *I am unhappy, frustrated, pessimistic, afraid.* Your subconscious mind, unable to distinguish between what you are telling it through your presleep conditioning ritual and what is actually happening in your everyday world, says to you, "Okay, I've got it."

Your thoughts are on what you do not want and what you despise, and your feelings in your body bring you worry, fear, anxiety, hate, sadness, and the like. Your subconscious mind responds with no desire to change your conscious waking state, because it only reacts to what you place there. So it will proceed to offer you experiences from the universal one subconscious mind that aligns with what you've programmed it to do. You placed your thoughts in your subconscious, when it would most likely have at least eight hours of sleep to work on them! The subconscious can't be faulted for assuming that you must want them very, very much.

Alas, you awaken befuddled by all of the things you don't want that keep showing up in your life, not understanding that by assuming the feeling of what you *don't* wish for and then going to sleep with those thoughts in your mind, you are programming your subconscious mind to take over, just as it did when you were first learning to drive. The difference is that then you were creating what you desired, and now you are using the same strategy to attract what you *do not desire*. And this is why you so often fail to attract the ideal in your life.

Neville puts it this way:

> Whatever you have in consciousness as you go to sleep is the measure of your expression in the waking two-thirds of your life on earth. Nothing stops you from realizing your objective, save your failure to feel that you are already that which you wish to be, or that you are already in possession of the thing sought. Your subconscious gives form to your desires only when you feel your wish fulfilled.[40]

You can train yourself to do this in the precious five minutes before slumber overtakes you.

If you decide you do not want to go to sleep with this first choice in your consciousness, you can develop a new habit for your habitual mind to latch onto. You do have an alternative—those last five minutes of the day are your five minutes and yours alone. Consider the second option using your last waking moments before sleep, programming your subconscious mind in a new way.

2. Choosing to Assume the Feeling of the Wish Fulfilled

As you lie in bed, feeling drowsy and knowing that you are about to go to sleep—where your subconscious mind is most at home—use these final preslumber moments to align with your Source of being and become a wishes fulfilled spiritual being.

In these presleep moments, you can program your subconscious mind to automatically present you with fulfilled wishes.

You wouldn't train your subconscious mind to repeatedly slam on the brakes or to make a turn into a driveway without safely slowing down. You also don't want to train your subconscious mind to focus on and attract the kinds of things that make you unhappy or create unnecessary pain. These last five minutes awake, then, are your final pep talk to your subconscious mind. You want to focus on assuming the feeling of the wish fulfilled that you've placed into your imagination.

Here's what Neville offers on this topic—it may be the most valuable information you've ever received:

> The feeling which comes in response to the question "How would I feel were my wish realized?" is the feeling which should monopolize and immobilize your attention as you relax into sleep. You must be in the consciousness of being or having that which you want to be or to have before you drop off to sleep.[41]

So this is what you must ask yourself as you get closer and closer to dropping off into the unconsciousness of sleep—*If my wishes were realized, how would it feel right here right now in my body?* Stay with that thought until you begin to feel your body shift into what that feels like.

This is not an empty exercise—it is a programming tool for reteaching your subconscious mind to act on what you intend to manifest, rather than on what you are worried, angry, or fearful about. In this semi-somnolent state, go to the *I am* that you are now putting into your imagination. For example, if you are worried about your health—whether because of a common cold, a pulled muscle, or a fearful diagnosis of a potentially life-threatening sickness—declare, "I am God in action." Or you could contemplate my favorite quotation from Saint Germain in *The "I AM" Discourses:*

> I want so much to have you feel that you are the Only Authority in this world or any other, so far as your world is concerned. Do not ever fear that the perfecting of your world is going

to disfigure anyone else's world, so long as your intent is not to harm anyone. It does not matter what the world about you says, or how much they try to intrude upon you their doubts, fears and limitations. You are the Supreme Authority in your world and all you have to do is to say, when you are beset by those conditions, "'I AM' the Mighty, Magic Circle of Protection about me that is Invincible and repels from me every discordant thought and element which seeks to find entrance or intrude itself. 'I AM' the Perfection of my world and it is Self-sustained."[42]

This is very powerful advice. When he says it does not matter what the world about you says, he is also talking about all of those self-limiting thoughts that you yourself have proclaimed regarding your ability to be healed.

As you lie in bed, affirm: *I am perfect health,* or use the words of Saint Germain above about being mighty and the perfection of your world—then notice how that feels in your body. At first you will be calling upon your ego, which believes that it is separate from God or the universal Source of all, and an inner voice will say, *This is silly, I am sick, I am sore, I am dying, and I am only fooling myself.* So simply dismiss these mind viruses and conditioned memes, since you are free to use these five minutes in any way that you choose.

Repeat a new *I am* that shifts you to the state of the realized wish. Repeatedly tell yourself that *I am God in action,* and immediately check in with your body to feel the shift from fear and anxiety to peace, love, and contentment. After a little practice, you will find that repeating *I am* in your mind begins to impact how you are feeling. Sensations of worry and pain slowly dissolve as you assume the feeling of the wish fulfilled, and it is at this point that you allow yourself to drop off to sleep.

Use these precious presleep moments to assume the feeling in your body of whatever wishes you desire as already fulfilled. Refuse to go to sleep being upset or disturbed about anything, regardless of how momentous it may appear to be in your life. The natural state of your subconscious is sleep, and it sees you as you believe yourself to be. It matters not to the habitual mind of yours whether what you believe and consequently feel in your body is harmful, moral, good, bad, or indifferent. It will faithfully take on your belief and provide you with an array of experiences and seemingly synchronistic events that give form to what you believe and have placed into the programming of your subconscious mind.

On many occasions I've gone to bed feeling somewhat sick or concerned about what course my body will take with its diagnoses. I've faithfully practiced what I am writing about, and I've awakened symptom-free. The key is to keep checking in with my body until I can say in all honesty that I'm feeling that my desire is a present fact. Feelings are the tools that the subconscious automatic mind uses.

You can quite readily break the habit of using your resting time before sleep reviewing things that are frustrating and upsetting. Make this a sacred satisfying time to nurture thoughts that align with the *I am* thoughts that you have placed into your imagination. When you see a tendency toward negativity, simply pause and gently remind yourself in your sleepy state that you do not wish to enter your unconscious world with these feelings. Then assume that feeling in your body of your wish fulfilled. You want to enter your sleep with reminders to your subconscious to automatically fulfill your life-enhancing wishes.

Your Subconscious Mind Never Sleeps

The validity of a universal subconscious mind that is the only one mind is a concept that ego struggles to understand. It is of the highest order of importance if you want to master the art of manifestation.

"This infinite intelligence, then, is the only mind there is; we are all using it; we can't help using it; for it is one and everywhere and is the stuff from which all things are made." This quote is from one of my favorite books: *Three Magic Words,* written by Uell S. Andersen, which I've referred to earlier in this book. This one universal mind is infinite in time, space, and substance; and as the author concludes, "One mind only, which is everywhere and everything; this is the Subconscious Mind." And finally here's a description of what takes place in the subconscious mind while you sleep: "In other words, this Subconscious Mind attempts to create in form and circumstance that which the Conscious Mind suggests to it." Contemplate these insights throughout your day and particularly before going to sleep.

Your conscious mind, as you go to sleep, is capable of impressing your great *I am* upon your subconscious mind, which is a sliver of the one all-creating subconscious mind. This one mind never sleeps because it is infinite and therefore everywhere and in everything—it is always in the process of creating and manifesting. Throughout those hours while your conscious mind is resting, your subconscious mind is receiving and processing all that you've downloaded into it, and getting ready to turn its impressions into form and circumstances.

In his book *The Biology of Belief,* my friend Bruce Lipton puts this phenomenon of the conscious and subconscious mind into the language of modern technology, using this metaphor: "In reality, the subconscious is an emotionless database of stored programs, whose function is strictly concerned with reading environmental signals and engaging in hardwired behavioral programs, no questions asked, no judgments made. The subconscious mind is a programmable 'hard drive' into which our life experiences are downloaded."

So here you are lying in your bed, about to enter into your unconscious state where your subconscious mind is most at home. In Lipton's analogy, there's a computer ready and waiting to get to work as soon as you doze off and leave your conscious mind behind. As you lie there, what you say to yourself as an *I am* is what you download into the computer. The computer I'm using to stand in for one universal subconscious mind is so vast that it has no beginning and no end and everything exists within it. If everything exists within it and it is infinite, that means *you* exist within it as well, and it must respond to what you load into it. It cannot sleep; it is too busy turning conscious impressions into form and circumstances. All you have to do is understand this power is within you and be in a state of gratitude for your highest self, which is God.

Remember those three magic words: *You are God.* There is only one subconscious mind, and your own subconscious mind is a part of that one mind. That invisible part of you is really the mind of God at work—as long as you don't edge God out (ego), which is what your conscious mind has probably been trained to do.

If your subconscious mind receives your conviction that you have money, you will have money. If it receives the conviction that *I am happy, I am healthy, I am content, I am love, I am wise,* or any other statement downloaded with conviction, the subconscious mind will bring it into your physical reality. I am not suggesting that you have *hope,* or tell yourself *maybe,* or use the last five minutes awake to say "I *will* be happy," "I *will* be prosperous," "I *hope to one day* be content." Use the name that God gave to Moses as he described who he is: *I am that I am.*

This is where faith plays a decisive role. You must extinguish any thought that being one with God is impossible. That is the false self at work—the contaminated personal subconscious that receives toxic self-limiting ideas and turns them into your unfulfilled reality. You are one with the one universal subconscious mind of God that never sleeps, and works for you while your conscious mind slumbers. You want it to work for you using what you download into it—even as you are in deep sleep.

While You Sleep, Your Subconscious Mind Works

One of my spiritual teachers, Omraam Mikhaël Aïvanhov—the Bulgarian mystic philosopher and teacher of the Universal White Brotherhood—has this to say about your preparation for sleep and what transpires while your sleep: "It is the experiences of the last minutes before you go to sleep that are more important, more significant, than everything that happened during the day." He speaks eloquently on the importance of entering the sub-conscious mind with a purity of spirit because each night we die—and if we don't know how to prepare for our nightly death, we will be unprepared for our true departure to the other world. "Take care, therefore," he urges us, "never to go to sleep with negative thoughts in your mind, for they will destroy all the good you may have gained during the day."

Your time while asleep, when you leave this house and yet are still attached to it, is to be thought of as a sacred journey that you take daily to connect to the one universal subconscious mind and experience the bewildering wonder of what transpires there. Once again, Aïvanhov tells us: "Before going to sleep, you must get ready as though for a sacred pilgrimage . . . never go to bed with a negative thought in your head, for it will wreak havoc in your subconscious." In those eight or so hours that you are embedded in your sub-conscious mind, you receive instruction. The feelings you brought to your sleep time will be expressed tomorrow and in all of your tomorrows. This is a time when you leave behind the constrictions of your physical world and the limitations of your physical body. You allow the one subconscious mind to create your wishes without active participation from your solid material self.

I cannot describe to you precisely how your subconscious mind works while you sleep, nor can anyone give you this kind of detail. As Neville puts it, "The subconscious receives impressions only through the feelings of man and in a way known only to itself gives these impressions form and expression."[43]

Who can describe the intricacies of a caterpillar weaving its own chrysalis and then emerging as a beautiful butterfly? It is a mystery known only to the one mind, as is how a subconscious impression turns into a hardened fact. But you can be cognizant of the many mysterious things you do while asleep, all the while believing them to be true and experiencing them in your body even though you are unconscious. I only ask you to enjoy the mysterious and know that it is full of potential. Wallow in it, and when you do, you open yourself up to infinite possibilities.

While asleep you dream, entering a totally unique dimension that feels absolutely real for all the time you're dreaming. During dream time, your subconscious mind takes over, presenting you with a magical world where everything occurs without your active participation. You don't have to get up and do anything, you don't need to move, and you don't need the assistance of anyone. You don't need money, luck, tools, transportation of any kind, your family, your church, an education, a book—nothing. It all takes place while your physical self is in bed, unconscious, out of your body—yet still attached to it. How does all of this stupendous manifestation take place, *in a way known only to itself?*

There are some things taking place while you slumber that might give you pause. One-third of your life is lived in a reality that offers you clues as to what is possible for you when you are in your dreams awake. You can get a glimmer of how the one universal subconscious mind works if you can look back, from a waking state, and examine what is taking place during the sleeping third of your life.

In your dream state, you are able to create anything that you desire simply by using your powers of thought to make it happen. You don't have to get out of bed, get dressed, set a goal and then an intention, go to a car dealership to test-drive the car you love, write a check, and drive away with your new purchase. All you need do is place the idea into your sleepy imagination, feel it in your body (your heart rate goes up, your breathing increases, you are feeling the joy in your smile), and *voilà!* There it is—you are driving in your new car. It is all very real, and all you had to do was have the thought, live from the end, and feel it. Your subconscious mind, now fully connected to the one subconscious mind, has allowed you to participate in the true art of manifestation. And as long as you stay in your dream state, unconscious in your slumber, "then He opens the ears of men, and seals their instructions," as it is revealed in the book of Job.

In Anita Moorjani's NDE report quoted earlier, she speaks about the absence of time, and the sensation that everything seemed to be happening at once. No time experience, only now.

And so it is in your dream state as well. You can be five years old and fifty years old all at the same time in your dream. You can be with the same person simultaneously alive and dead in your dream.

Albert Einstein's study of quantum physics was devoted to the simple message that we live in a completed universe, and that time is an invention of man and essentially an illusion. Anita's NDE unconscious state reinforces Einstein's idea of no time. Anita said that past lives did not exist in those moments. Everything was happening now. The only way she could describe it was that what we call past lives appeared to be *parallel* lives, and that everything was simply all one. In your unconscious sleep state, you can be anything and everything; you can be yourself and someone else or something else—even an animal—simultaneously. Linearity seems to disappear. Anything that you can imagine is yours. Nothing is impossible. Want to fly? Then imagine it and feel it, and off you go.

While asleep and dreaming, you're not restricted to cause and effect. In your dreaming body you can come and go as you please. Things do not have to follow the same rules that seem to apply to your waking world. If you imagine and feel it as a present-moment fact, it is there for you instantaneously. Everything you need for the dream is created by you in harmony with your subconscious mind. You don't have to do anything but allow your thoughts to create what they desire and to feel it in your sleeping body.

Think about all of the things that take place in the one-third of your life while you sleep. There is no time, no cause and effect —everything you experience is created by your imagination. The people and events are all illusions, simply figments of your imagination. There is no beginning and no end, no linear progression, and it all seems to make perfect sense as long as you're in the dream state.

I'm reminded of Henry David Thoreau's observation that "Our truest life is when we are in dreams awake." It seems only logical to me that if during one-third of our life on planet Earth, we are capable of manifesting anything that we place our attention on—without having to expend any physical effort, only by allowing ourselves to transcend time and space—then why not in the other two-thirds of our life? This is what I believe Thoreau is suggesting when he urges us to be true to our authentic self by being a waking dreamer.

As you look back at it from your "awakened" state, the time while you are in deep slumber provides you clues as to what is possible when you begin to awaken from this dream as well. You have experienced oneness, timelessness, miracle-making, and having your wishes fulfilled instantaneously for one-third of your life. Become a waking dreamer and begin to apply this same awareness to the entirety of your life. All of the things I have written throughout this book, you are capable of achieving while asleep. Make them your personal reality in all of your waking hours as well.

Remember, the only way you can be sure you were dreaming is to awaken. If you never awakened, it would all be the unlimited reality of your dream state. And so it is with the two-thirds of your life as well. The only way you will ever know you were dreaming is to revive while you are still alive, and look back at your dream from this awakened perspective. Remind yourself that you can indeed do as Thoreau suggests and find your truest self by being in your dreams awake.

Neville offers you these words on what takes place while you sleep:

> Sleep is the door through which the conscious, waking mind passes to be creatively joined to the subconscious. Sleep conceals the creative act while the objective world reveals it. In sleep man impresses the subconscious with his conception of himself.[44]

Each night as I drift off to sleep, I adamantly refuse to use this precious time to review anything that I do not want to be reinforced in the hours of being immersed in my subconscious mind. I choose to impress upon my subconscious mind, and therefore the mind of God to which I am eternally joined, my conception of myself as a Divine creator in alignment with the one mind. I groggily reiterate my *I ams*, which I have placed in my imagination, and I remember that my slumber will be dominated by my last waking concept of myself. *I am peaceful, I am content, I am love, I am writing, I am the governing power of the universe, and I attract only to myself those who are in alignment with my highest ideals of myself.*

This is my nightly ritual, always eschewing any temptation to go over any fear of unpleasantness that my ego might be asking me to review. I assume the feeling in my body of those *I am* statements already fulfilled, and I enter my sleep inviting the instruction that my subconscious mind welcomes. I know that I'm allowing myself to be programmed while asleep, for the next day I rise knowing that I am a free agent. I understand that every action and event of the day is essentially predetermined by my feelings as I prepared for sleep, and while I was in that place of warmth and trust in the arms of the one universal subconscious mind.

Waking Up

It is my intention to live in my dreams awake, as much as is humanly and spiritually conceivable. I look back upon my dream state, and I realize that everything that I needed for my dream I was able to create with my subconscious mind—without effort, and with no need for involving my physical body at all. And so I know that manifesting the person I wish to be while awake also involves effortless perfection and that I have my imagination—or my intentions, my attention, and my feelings—to use while awake as well. My sleep time fully embedded in my subconscious mind is providing clues for me to put those mental activities into practice when I leave my slumber.

I further look back at my dream time from a place of wakefulness, and I see that everything and everyone that was in my dream was created by me with my imagination. I keep this in mind as I gaze at who and what I have created in my awake dream. I look back from my wakeful perspective and realize that I lived in a world where time is an illusion, where nothing is unavailable to me, where cause and effect are total illusions, where all obstacles are turned into either opportunities or revealed as illusions, where there is no beginning and no end, and where my body experiences feelings even though the thoughts that resulted in those feelings are all illusions and were totally devoid of judgments by my dreaming self.

And finally, I look back and realize that the only way I know for certain that I was dreaming was to awaken. I remind you here as well that you do have within you these amazing powers of manifestation, and you use them on a regular basis every night and for one-third of your entire time in this incarnation. I suggest that while you are awake, you view this two-thirds portion of your life as a dream as well, and realize that the only way you'll know you are dreaming is to awaken. Awaken to a new consciousness in which distance and time constraints can be overcome just by a change of state. An awakened state that knows and trusts in the power of your thoughts and feelings to live a wishes fulfilled life.

In all of your waking hours, I encourage you to stay closely aligned to your originating Source of being. Practice thinking like God (your highest self) thinks. As I pointed out in a previous book, *Excuses Begone!*, when your contemplations are a vibrational match to originating Spirit, you are synchronized with Divine mind, attracting and fulfilling your desires. You have the same power as originating Spirit, as long as you don't replace your Divine nature with ego's thoughts, which are essentially the mental meanderings of your false self.

While awake, use your mind to repeatedly remind yourself of your true *I am that I am* nature. Remember that universal one subconscious mind creates in a way known only to itself. It is the great mystery. Learn to live in that mystery, making every effort to use all of your mental and feeling powers to manifest the life you desire, all the while staying in an uncompromised state of love. Here is what Erich Fromm wrote on this subject of living the mystery: "Rather than be confronted with an overwhelming proof of the limitations of our understanding, we accuse the dreams of not making sense."

You needn't be concerned with how it will all work out; all you need to know is that you are always connected to your Source of being, and that you and God are truly one. Just as no scientist can tell you how a caterpillar knows how to turn itself into a butterfly and then migrate thousands of miles without the benefit of a brain, you must simply accept the great mystery of life and death and stay as closely aligned with this miraculous thing we call creative Source of all being as you possibly can. You don't have to understand it all; all you need do is remain in a state of love while reprogramming your subconscious mind to develop the habits of a God-realized being, rather than an ego-dominated person.

As the Lebanese poet Kahlil Gibran observed in his classic book *The Prophet,* "Trust the dreams, for in them is hidden the gate to eternity." I urge you to follow the poet's advice and open up that gate and come to know a new external you, in your dreams awake, and never forget your own Divine magnificence.

Three Suggestions

— As you lie in bed preparing for your nightly slumber, remember that the last thought you have in your mind can last up to four hours in your subconscious mind. That's four hours of programming from just one moment of contemplation prior to going into your unconscious state. Create a reminder like a prayer or mantra to place by your bed. Write these words and read them as you get comfortable: *I am going to use these moments to review what I intend to manifest into my life.* Keep that sign there to remind you how to spend your presleep moments nightly.

— Reproduce this quotation from Saint Germain in *The "I AM" Discourses* and repeat it at least three times as you prepare to go to sleep as a daily/nightly reminder that you are sending forth the greatest decree possible: "'I AM' the Governing Presence, governing in Perfect Divine Order, commanding Harmony, Happiness, and the Presence of God's Opulence in my mind, my home, and my world."[45] Make a serious effort to feel the sustaining power of this in your body.

— If before dropping off to sleep you are assailed by worry, distress, or fear, do not stay in bed. Get up, turn on the light, take a few deep breaths, read from a spiritual text, meditate for a few moments in front of a white candle, say a prayer—do anything other than staying there lying down. You cannot defend yourself against these onslaughts while remaining snug in your bed. If distressing feelings come back when you return to bed, get up, turn on the lights, and try something else. When you finally do feel peaceful back in bed, repeat the *I ams* from suggestions one and two on the previous page and drift off to sleep ready to have *your ears opened and your instructions sealed.*

MAKING IT ALL
COME TOGETHER

*"Turn back to the higher planes and plunge into
the cosmic ocean once again . . . People think that
it is in the details that they will find the light,
the precision, they are looking for, but this is an
illusion: you will find far more light in what is vague
and indistinct . . . The human soul needs immensity;
only in immensity can it be happy and feel free to breathe."*

— OMRAAM MIKHAËL AÏVANHOV

This final chapter will assist you in achieving that immensity
that your soul is seeking. It is comprised of seven questions for you
to contemplate and explore as you begin your wishes fulfilled life.
The questions are based on the five wishes fulfilled foundations
and the three opening chapters.

These questions, along with my ideas and suggestions, are in
no particular order of importance—they are offered in the hope
that as you finish reading this book, you have a strong aura of *all
things are possible* swirling around in your consciousness. Once you

decide to live from this Divine awareness, your life takes on an air of appreciation for the mysterious and a belief in the miraculous. All of your God-realized wishes will indeed be fulfilled.

Question #1: Does It Feel Natural?

There will be times when you doubt your ability to attract into life the successful fulfillment of your wishes, including the ideal person you would like to be. I realize these words appear to contradict what I've written earlier in this book. However, I'm addressing this question from the position of the overly conditioned ego that's been trained to believe it's preposterous to think you can become what you would like to be by simply assuming the feeling in your body of your wishes being fulfilled.

Neville alerts you to this disruptive influence with these words:

> The time it takes your assumption to become fact, your desire to be fulfilled, is directly proportionate to the naturalness of your feeling of already being what you want to be—of already having what you desire.
>
> The fact that it does not feel *natural* to you to be what you imagine yourself to be is *the secret of your failure*. Regardless of your desire, regardless of how faithfully and intelligently you follow the law, if you do not feel *natural* about what you want to be, *you will not be it.*[46]

Think about what you plan to manifest—then use your imagination to feel what that feels like in your body. Does it feel natural to you? I mean, does it really feel like this is the you that you are deciding to be? If you've been sickly for most of your life and you are assuming the feeling of a healthy body, does it feel natural to see yourself as a picture of perfect health? Do you feel that with your imagination and God, all things are possible? If you've been overweight, or addicted, or poor, or victimized, or unlucky, or weak, or anything at all that is incongruous with your perfect well-being, can you feel natural when you assume the feeling of your new ideal?

Do you feel entitled to prosperity, health, happiness? If that feels unnatural, you must take on this task that Neville defines in this way: "The essential feeling of naturalness can be achieved by *persistently filling your consciousness with imagination*—imagining yourself being what you want to be or having what you desire."[47]

I readily admit that there are some things that you might desire or wish for that will never feel natural to you. This came up in an interview I recently did on a telecast for a national television network. The interviewer asked, "Do you mean to tell me, Dr. Dyer, that if I do all that you recommend, and follow the Law of Assumption to the letter, I can become a linebacker for the New York Giants?" Now this man was about 5 feet 7 inches tall and weighed maybe 150 pounds—a small man imagining himself in a very large man's physical position on a professional football team.

I asked him, "Does it feel natural for you to be playing that position on the Giants?" His immediate response was, "Not at all." And thus, I reminded him that *the time it takes your assumption to become reality is proportionate to the naturalness of being it.*

In my opinion, the interviewer would be doomed to failure with his assumption. However, I've seen professional basketball players who were 5 feet 7 inches tall, in a profession populated by giants—and not only could they play at an all-star level, but they could jump high enough to dunk a basketball. When interviewed, they said without hesitation, "It feels natural to me, even though no one else can imagine it happening."

This is relevant to you, because it's actually rare to desire what simply feels unnatural. If being healthy, prosperous, happy, successful, strong, intelligent, and so on feel unnatural, then naturalness may be achieved by persistently using your imagination and your subjective attention to make this feeling stick.

Throughout my life it's felt natural to achieve prosperity, heal my body, teach self-reliance, and simply be happy. When I was a schoolteacher, most people said (and I still hear it to this day), "You can't make any money as a schoolteacher; after all it's a low-paying profession." Yet being prosperous and making money has always seemed natural to me.

When I was a schoolteacher, I taught extra courses at night school, worked every summer, started a driver-education business, gave public lectures for a fee on Monday nights, became a consultant on how to attract government grants, started a tutoring business, wrote books, took additional college credits to maximize my salary, and on and on. Eventually, because it all felt so natural to me, I made teaching a very lucrative profession. At one time I was restricted to a classroom as a teacher; today I'm still a teacher, only my classroom has now become the entire globe.

Whatever it is that you want to manifest for yourself, do not be afraid to place it into your imagination, assume the feeling of that wish fulfilled, and by all means, make it feel as natural as apple pie.

Today we have a man who elevated his life to become the President of the United States. Given his position in life—as the child of a mixed-race marriage, raised partially in a Muslim country, with the name of Barack Hussein Obama—virtually everyone would have said that this young boy's aspirations were unnatural, plain and simple. But he didn't see it that way, and neither should you.

Move your highest dreams to a rightful natural place in your imagination, and then do as Ralph Waldo Emerson, the man whose portrait I'm looking at as I write, advised: "Build, therefore, your own world. As fast as you conform your life to the pure idea in your mind, that will unfold its great proportions."

It is my long-held strong belief and knowing that you are never given the power to dream without the equivalent power to manifest that dream and make it your physical reality. And this is also from Emerson to chew on: "Every spirit builds itself a house; and beyond its house a world; and beyond its world, a heaven. Know then, that the world exists for you. For you is the phenomenon perfect. What are we, that only can we see."

Question #2: Am I Willing to Command My I Am Presence?

It is totally unnecessary for you to be subtle or obsequious with your highest self. You are God—not the ego-oriented model of a deity superior to everyone and everything, but the God Who is spoken of in the New Testament: "He who does not love does not know God, for God is love" (1 John 4:8), and "We are of God" (1 John 4:6). Therefore, as long as you stay in a state of love, you must be God—"and everyone who loves is born of God and knows God" (1 John 4:7). This is not the concept of God that you were probably raised with, even though this couldn't be more clearly delineated in the scriptures of virtually all faiths.

View your *I am* presence as an invisible energy residing within and around you at all times, which is yours to use as you see fit. It is not an external power residing out there somewhere that you can't see or touch, or that you must beg to serve you—it is your very highest self. I encourage you to make use of this God-power by insisting upon it serving you in the manifestation of your highest aspirations for yourself and all of humanity.

In *The "I AM" Discourses,* Saint Germain says it this way: "Therefore, when you say: 'I AM the Conquering Presence! I command this I AM Presence to govern perfectly my mind, home, affairs and world,' you have sent forth the greatest Decree possible to be given."[48] Notice the word *command.* This is in sharp distinction to the teachings that counsel us to treat God gingerly in our prayers and discussions, to be careful not to insult God, and to be fearful of Him.

I'm not suggesting you adopt an attitude of arrogance in your relationship with the Source of all being—that would contradict the quote from the book of John, that God is love. This second question is about you having absolute faith in your own *I am* presence and a willingness to be insistent on the cooperation of the God force—to which you are eternally connected because you are of God.

When you place an intention in your imagination, do not allow a question mark at the end of your pronouncement. See your statement ending in a grammatical exclamation point. "I bring this into my reality!" is easy to say if you're already living from that declaration in your imagination and have assumed the feeling in your body of that wish being fulfilled.

As Saint Germain advises, "Put all your power back with God, and then when you command—no matter what it is you want— you have all power instantly on hand to bring forth the fulfillment of your Decree."⁴⁹ Another favorite observation from *The "I AM" Discourses* is this: "Say to your Divine Self: 'See here, God! come forth and take care of this.' God wants you to set Him to work. This releases a flood of the God-Energy, Intelligence and Substance which flows forth to do the command."⁵⁰

Here's one final offering from *The "I AM" Discourses* regarding your insistence on having your physical body live from a place of Divine perfection and well-being: "You must take the unconditional stand with your body that: '"The I AM Presence" governs this physical body completely and compels it into obedience.' The more attention you give your body, the more it is the master, and the more it will demand and keep demanding from you."⁵¹ And then to bring this point home to you, Saint Germain offers you these encouraging words regarding your ability to have the *I am* commanding presence work for your perfect health: "You can positively produce whatever you want in your body if you will fix your attention upon the Perfection of it—but do not let your attention rest on its imperfections."⁵²

If what I am writing here makes you feel a bit squeamish, ask yourself why in the world would you feel threatened by commanding your God-presence to go to work for you? Do you believe that God is truly love as it is reported over and over in all of the spiritual texts, particularly the New Testament, the Koran, the Bhagavad Gita, and the Tao Te Ching?

Be persistent in the use of your *I am* presence. More than that—be *insistent* and command your highest self to set in motion all of the forces of creation that will result in the hardening into fact that which you have placed into your imagination as an already realized fact. I want to *reemphasize* that commanding your *I am* presence to manifest your heart's desire is not in any way contemptuous or arrogant.

If you are not coming from a place of radical humility, then you have invested your efforts in your ego—and that means, of course, that you have edged God out of the entire process. Insisting upon your highest self serving you in the act of manifestation means that you have absolute, total faith and conviction in your intention. It is much like your everyday act of breathing, eating, beating your heart, and digesting your food. Of course you are in a profound state of gratitude for all of these, and millions more, everyday miracles. And at the same time you demand and insist upon everything that is involved in all of these activities. You are enabled to obey the original fiat of God, as reported in the book of Genesis, to take dominion over the earth. Taking dominion means that you insist on it—and remember at all times that you can ask that *love* take dominion over you and the entire world.

Be in a deep state of gratitude for all that you are currently experiencing and all that you are in the process of manifesting, and remain humble for all that comes your way. At the same time, be 100 percent insistent upon having your wishes fulfilled with the Divine assistance of your spiritual Source of being. Simply *know*, beyond all doubt, that your desires are in the midst of hardening into objects, circumstances, facts, and events—along with a new, Divinely inspired you—as long as those desires are consistent with the third question that you are about to ponder.

Question #3: Are My Wishes in Alignment with My Highest Self?

This principle invites you to choose which possibility you identify with and, as has been stressed throughout this book, to live as if it has already occurred. If you place into your imagination wishes that are misaligned with your highest God-realized self, you will find yourself frustrated and immobilized. *God is love*—if your aspirations in any way are outside of this mantra, you will feel lost and you will not succeed.

If God is one, then God is incapable of being divided. If your desires involve conflict for yourself or anyone else, then you have brought two into the picture: that is yourself, as well as the second party who might be harmed by the fulfillment of your wish. God, being only oneness wherein all things are connected, and God (your highest self) being love cannot even recognize the dichotomy that you bring to the picture. If God acknowledged a desire that would bring harm to anyone, God wouldn't and couldn't be God. How could that which is all one recognize two (which is needed in order to have conflict) and still be God?

This is what happens when you attempt to manifest from a place of selfishness or potential harm to anyone else. You invoke the ego, which is always about winning, overpowering, being better than others, accumulating for the sake of feeling superior, achieving for adulation or recognition, improving your status, and so on. And again—ego is edging God out. I love the way Neville speaks to this point: "You never draw out of the deep of yourself that which you want; you always draw that which you are, and you are that which you feel yourself to be as well as that which you feel is true of others."[53] So in this manifestation activity, the secret is to feel yourself as already being and having what you desire, and to keep the entirety of it all wrapped up in a spirit of love.

By all means place into your imagination the idea of living a prosperous life, but this in no way implies from a God-realized position that you desire a fancy watch, a luxury automobile, a large infusion of cash, a palatial home, or anything else that is for the purpose of elevating your position among your peers. This immediately involves conflict—twoness—you and those you are attempting to impress with your being in some way superior. Staying aligned with your Source of being means no one is, in any way, better than anyone else regardless of the monetary value of their stuff.

This third question is asking if you love as you are loved by the creative Source of all. Can you ask out of love, live and feel as if what you desire is already a present fact, and then allow the universal Source of all to provide, with no concern about appeasing the demands of your ego?

If demanding and insisting is your style, do it from a place of pure love. Be willing to give it all away in the name of that love. Stay in that place of pure humility. If you desire to purify your body and live from a disease-free place of perfect health, simply assume the feeling of love throughout your body and live as if it were your reality. Not to impress others, not to have special privileges bestowed upon you because you are more special and thus more deserving of this healing, but purely out of your humble sense of gratitude for being in a state of well-being.

Albert Einstein once famously observed that all he wanted to do was to learn to think like God thinks. This means living and manifesting from a place of all-encompassing desire to serve others, to be love, to ask nothing in return for what you give; in other words, to simply be love. Get your ego out of the picture and "draw out of the deep of yourself," as Neville expresses it. And the "deep of yourself" is truly your highest self, which is of course God. Let the God that you are, the God that Jesus said you are, the God that is your very essence, your deepest self—let this be the energy you draw upon to fill your imagination, and then know that you are fully aligned with the only Source that is responsible for all of creation.

As you begin to see your Divinely aligned manifestations show up in your physical world, think like God thinks and share any munificence with others with no expectation of anything back, including even a thank-you if it is not forthcoming. As you place your intentions into your imagination and assume the feeling of those intentions being fulfilled, ask not for anything that is outside the great umbrella of love that is God.

The words of Jesus in the book of Luke sum up all that I am saying here:

But if you love those who love you, what credit is that to you? For even sinners love those who love them. And if you do good to those who do good to you, what credit is that to you? For even sinners do the same. . . . But love your enemies, do good, and lend, hoping for nothing in return; and your reward will be great, and you will be sons of the Most High. For He is kind to the unthankful and evil. Therefore be merciful, just as your Father also is merciful (Luke 6:32–36).

Similarly, Lao-tzu, some six centuries or so earlier, reminds you that the great sage is kind to the kind, and kind to the unkind, because kindness is his nature.

If you can make your desires harmonize with the messages of the above passage, while practicing humility and keeping your ego at bay, you will come to see the truth in Neville's observation that "You never draw out of the deep of yourself that which you want; you always draw that which you are." The key here is "the deep of yourself"—that is your highest self, and you will also see the significance of the fourth question, which follows.

Question #4: Am I Free of Judgment, Condemnation, and Criticism?

Several months ago, my desire to manifest something into my life did not appear to be registering with the God force that brings all things into being. It is not that I was being impatient, for I have come to know in my heart of hearts that all things arrive in Divine time and that it is not the job of my ego to say when what I desire should show up. I have come to fully accept that "Infinite patience produces immediate effects" as *A Course in Miracles* tells us. The immediate results are the sense of inner peace that I feel when I trust in the Divine, and infinite patience is just another way of saying *pure faith*.

The point I'm making here is that I wasn't experiencing anything remotely close to inner contentment. In fact, the more I focused on what it was that I wished to see fulfilled—even though

I was practicing everything that I've written here in the first eight chapters of this book—the more I felt anxious, sad, worried, frustrated, and even mildly angry at times. It just didn't seem to be working.

Then one day I was rereading for the umpteenth time the third volume of *The "I AM" Discourses*—the little book that was left at the yoga studio all wrapped up in gold and that influenced the creation of this book. And I came upon something that made me realize why my feelings in my body were so discordant when it came to the fulfillment of one of my greatest wishes:

> The student should constantly look within his human self and see what habits or creations are there that need to be plucked out and disposed of; for only by refusing to any longer allow habits of judging, condemning and criticizing to exist can he be free. The true activity of the student is only to perfect his own world, and he cannot do it as long as he sees imperfection in the world of another of God's children.[54]

Reading this paragraph was like having a bucket of cold water thrown in my face, to shock me from the coma that had defined my life in relation to the lack of fulfillment of my wishes regarding this particular thing (which I choose to have remain private). All the while I was using my imagination to have a clear picture of what I wanted, I practiced living from that mental position, I assumed the feeling of the wish fulfilled, I used my subjective attention to keep that vision alive in my inner world, and I always used the last few moments of my awake time to go over and over what I wished to manifest before entering my unconscious state of sleep where my subconscious mind was most at home.

During all that time, I was also seeing imperfection in another of God's children. I lovingly criticized, not so lovingly condemned, and my judgments frequently overshadowed my spiritual visualizations and intentions. I had to learn that every single one of God's children is doing what they know how to do, and I need to be able to love them, all of them, as our Source of being loves them. *Without judgment, without condemnation, and without criticism.*

If I'm to be a being of love living from my highest self, that means that love is all I have inside of me and all that I have to give away. If someone I love chooses to be something other than what my ego would prefer, I must send them the ingredients of my highest self, which is God, and God is love, as I have reiterated over and over throughout the pages of this book.

My criticism and condemnation of the thoughts, feelings, and behavior of others—regardless of how right and moral my human self convinces me it is—is a step away from God-realization. And it is God-consciousness that allows for my wishes to be fulfilled, as long as they are aligned with my Source of being.

I can come up with a long list of reasons why I should be judgmental and condemnatory toward another of God's children and why, damn it, I am right. Yet if I want to perfect my own world—and I so want to do so—then I must substitute love for these judgments, or take the consequences of not having my wishes fulfilled.

I spent years studying the teachings of Patanjali, and he reminded us several thousand years ago that when we are steadfast—which means that we never slip in our abstention of thoughts of harm directed toward others—then all living creatures cease to feel enmity in our presence. Now I know that we are all human: you, me, all of us. We do occasionally slip and retreat from our highest self into judgment, criticism, and condemnation, but this is not a rationale for choosing to practice that kind of interaction.

I can only tell you that when I finally got it, and I sent only love to another of God's children whom I had been judging and criticizing, I got the immediate result of inner contentment—and my wishes have definitely, assuredly, been fulfilled. I urge you to send love in place of those judgments and criticisms to others when you feel they impede your joy and happiness, and hold them in that place of love. Notice that if you stay steadfast, when you change the way you look at things, the things you look at do change.

Question #5: Do I Pray as If My Prayers Are Already Realized?

The traditional means of prayer that I was exposed to throughout my life involved asking for something and hoping that an external God would provide me with the answers for my wishes.

A close friend and colleague, Gregg Braden, who is also a student and admirer of Neville, writes in his penetrating book *The Isaiah Effect:*

> Rather than *asking* that the outcome of our prayer come to pass, we acknowledge our role as an active part of creation and give thanks for what we are certain that we have created. Whether we see immediate results or not, our thanks acknowledge that somewhere in creation our prayer has already been fulfilled.

This may appear to contradict the "Ask and you shall receive" version of prayer that you were likely exposed to. It may feel new, but it is so important that you acknowledge your own Divine role in the fulfillment of your spiritually aligned desires for yourself and others.

A vision is within your imagination as you enter into your sacred practice of prayer, one that is so strong you can already feel its fulfillment in your own body. To once again quote Neville: "The moment you accept the wish as an accomplished fact the subconscious finds means for its realization. To pray successfully then, you must yield to the wish, that is, feel the wish fulfilled."[55]

Being a piece of God, and therefore altogether God as a part of the entire process of creation, you become an active participant in your own private prayerful moments. Consider shutting out your *senses* completely, along with all of the evidence they continually place before you—because you are, in your prayers, going to attempt to *feel* what they (your senses) will most assuredly deny. Perhaps describing what I do will help you.

When I pray I always yield to the wish that I have for myself, my loved ones, and the entire planet and all of its inhabitants, rather than attempting to force my wish or to have God take over and do my bidding for me. In my mind I see my wishes as accomplished, and I experience what that feels like, savoring the feeling in my body. I stay in a profound state of gratitude. My prayer is without effort; rather, it is felt as an already accomplished fact.

I then act as if what it is I am praying for is my truth, even if my senses and all of those about me give evidence to the contrary. I am not asking for special favors, because I do not believe in an ego-constructed deity who plays favorites, or has the ability to heal everyone yet withholds these favors because he or she is looking for something from me. I am a part of the entire business of creation. I am Divine consciousness and I never forget it. I know I have the capacity to make conscious contact with my source of creation—there's no fear of insulting a mythical god.

In *The "I AM" Discourses*, Saint Germain says, "I say to the students in all sincerity, there is no possible way of attaining a quality or a desired attribute without claiming it."[56] With this in mind, I claim peace, health, happiness, joy, prosperity for everyone I know in my life. I claim peace and contentment for myself, for humankind, and the entire world. In my prayers, I give thanks for my mysterious role in all of this, and I reprogram my subconscious mind so I feel this in my body. I leave my sacred prayer time and go about the activities of my life, whatever they may be, with this feeling within me. I am not discouraged by what my senses might be reporting. I have left all ideas of time and timing behind, and I trust in the *I am* presence that is my true identity.

Often at night I engage in prayerful visualization. I visualize faces of people I know who have crossed over and left the outer world, people I've seen in the media but have never met, and people I knew as a child. I surround them with love. I see the love, and I feel it for them and myself—I am calling in the *I am* presence.

As *The "I AM" Discourses* teach, "The undesirable moves out and the 'I AM presence' moves in; and you find that you have truly entered into a new world, filled with the Happiness and Perfection you have always known existed somewhere within your own heart."[57] This is prayer to me, and when I emerge from these moments of prayer, it is as if I have attended a movie and seen the successful end of the film, even though I may not have been shown precisely how that ending was achieved.

This is not only the great power of prayer, it is also the power of a wishes fulfilled life. No ego, no force, no special privileges; simply an awareness of the power that exists within us when we assume that what we pray for, always aligned with our highest selves, is a completed fact. We are, each and every one of us, a participant in this dance of creation.

Question #6: Is My Mind Open to Infinite Possibilities?

You live in an infinite universe that includes all of existence. Because this field is unlimited in dimension, nothing can happen outside of it. Everything that occurs within this field is completely influenced by it, and consequently, nothing accidental is possible. This field of consciousness—and your role in it—is, as I stated at the beginning of this book, omniscient, almighty, omnipresent, and a fragment of God. "With God all things are possible," which is infinitely exciting when you are convinced that means there's nothing left out.

Living from this perspective, if your wishes align with this one universal God force, miraculous occurrences become the norm. The universe seems to conspire in ways that are hidden from your intellectually inquiring mind, which seeks specific scientific answers as to why this or that seems to be taking place. While your cognitive apparatus remains totally befuddled, mysteriously benevolent forces begin to come to your aid. Synchronistic, unexplainable happenings become more easily accepted, and things that you were taught are impossible and outside the realm of reality show up.

I've had to address this question of being open to infinite possibilities during some meaningful and unanticipated events in my recent life. Since I've been practicing what I've written about throughout this book, and living from this God perspective,

I've experienced many things and events that I probably would have rejected without this awareness. Then again, I very likely wouldn't have been able to permit these new awarenesses to penetrate my ego-dominated shell.

I am choosing three examples of my personal experiences that have recently occurred as I've progressed on this path—as a man, a teacher, and a spiritual being.

The First Personal Experience

As I reported earlier in this book, there have been a significant number of unexplainable orbs showing up in photographs taken of me, particularly when I'm speaking before audiences on the subject matter that comprises the totality of the information in this book. Similarly, these orbs have also been appearing in photographs when I'm surrounded by people at these events—either signing books or simply enjoying the loving, friendly, and compassionate conversation that occurs at these gatherings. I have no idea what these orbs are, why they appear now and apparently haven't at earlier times, or if they have any hidden meanings. (See photo insert.)

I have read Klaus and Gundi Heinemann's book *Orbs: Their Mission and Messages of Hope,* and I encourage you to do the same. They've included their commentary on many photographs taken of these orbs at various functions throughout the world. Klaus holds a Ph.D. in experimental physics and has taught at Stanford University, and his wife is a respected educator in California. Obviously, these are thoughtful, informed people, whose inquiry into this phenomenon comes from a well-grounded perspective.

The orbs began appearing in my life recently during speeches and subsequent conversational groups. They seem to me to coincide with my decision to help myself and others live from a higher place of God-realization through exploring, living, and writing about aspects of God-consciousness.

If you look at the pictures of the orbs in this book's photo insert carefully, you see that a larger one appears above my head, and often the room is filled with smaller orbs, almost as a confirmation that the messages of love that infiltrate the occasion are being witnessed by these mysterious circles of light. I do not pretend to know what they are or why they are now making themselves known to me in the manner that they are appearing in my life. They could be emanations from spirit beings that could be surrounding me with new energy to heighten my awareness and help me to clarify my messages. I have no idea—all I know for certain is that *all things are possible,* and I'm open to what they may or may not be about.

My friend Linda Millek first acquainted me with these photographic light emanations during a Hay House Caribbean cruise not long ago. She told me that 18 years ago, her son had died while saving a friend in an auto accident. Her son communicates with her in a channeling fashion, and circular orbs and other orb shapes appear in her photos when she feels he's close to her. As she was telling me this, she said she could feel his presence there on the ship docked at St. Maarten. She took my picture, and there on my left and right hips was a megaphone-shaped orb identical to the ones she had seen in photos at her home. It was on this cruise that the first orb appeared, which I wrote about earlier in this book. (See photo insert.)

While I reiterate that I do not pretend to have an intelligent explanation for the continuing appearance of these orbs in my life, I love what Saint Ignatius of Loyola once told his followers: "For those who believe, no words are necessary. For those who do not believe, no words are possible." I leave you to make up your own mind, and I remain open to learning more about these mysterious occurrences.

The Second Personal Experience

My second example that defies any rational explanation involves my recent experience with a man who lives in the small village of Abadiania in Brazil. He goes by the name John of God. My friend Rayna Piskova, a medical doctor and eye surgeon who lives in California, has visited John of God in Brazil on several occasions. She asked me to go with her to receive his healing after learning of my diagnosis of leukemia. I agreed to go to Abadiania with her, but as the time approached, I made the decision to stay here in America, largely because I felt so compelled to write this book. I needed uninterrupted time to do the work of sitting down and disciplining myself each and every day for several months in order to complete the manuscript for the book you are now reading.

Rayna spent two weeks at the casa where John of God performs his surgeries. Although her original reason for going to Abadiania was for my healing, she received a surgical procedure herself. While there she sent a message asking that I have four photographs taken of me. I was instructed to dress in white outer garments and have the pictures taken from both sides, and from the front and back. On Friday she presented them to John of God and asked if he would allow surgery on me from these photos and from the long distance between Brazil and Hawaii where I was writing. John of God looked at the photos and said that he could not do the surgery because I needed to be taking special herbs, and without them it would be futile.

Rayna, God bless this Divine angel of a woman, doctor, and friend, obtained the special herbs, and then took them in a cab to a FedEx station. When they arrived three days later, I was told to take eight capsules over a 48-hour period, then have the photos retaken in white and e-mailed to her immediately. My daughter Serena took the four photos and e-mailed them to Rayna. The next day Rayna called and excitedly told me that John of God had agreed to participate in the surgery. It would be performed Thursday at 7 A.M. (2 P.M. in Brazil), and she gave me very specific instructions on what I was to do in preparation for the surgery.

At 7 A.M. that Thursday, I was in bed while this long-distance activity took place using the new photos. I was open-minded, yet I must confess that a smidgen of perplexity and skepticism wafted over me at this unusual transmission of long-distance surgery requiring four photos of me dressed in white, and that I swallow herb capsules FedExed from Brazil!

My cell phone began buzzing with messages from Rayna. I was to go back to bed and sleep for the next 24 hours. Eat no pepper, pork, or spicy foods. No exercise, no phones, no writing, no sex, and no massages for seven days when the sutures were to be removed. My first reaction was that I couldn't go back to sleep for 24 straight hours, as I had just awoken from 8 solid hours of sleep. Rayna told me that if I couldn't sleep, I was to *pretend* that I was sleeping, and the entities who do the healing would anesthetize me. Within five minutes I felt overwhelming fatigue. I lay down in bed and stayed there for the next 24 hours, only getting up twice to eat something light and to pee.

The next day, the idea of doing my normal routine of walking, swimming, stair-climbing, and weight lifting—which I've done daily for the past 35 years—seemed totally out of sync with what I was feeling. Even walking a few steps took my breath away. When I spoke to Rayna about this, she said, "You have had surgery. You absolutely must rest for the next seven days, or you will mess up everything that John of God has done for you."

So the entire week passed, and my daughter Serena simply took care of me while I did nothing but rest. My body was detoxifying in a very big way. I went from feeling just fine to coughing up phlegm and having flu-like symptoms, difficulty breathing, exhaustion, watery eyes, and many other symptoms. Exercising in any way was totally out of the question. I spent one week in a total state of rest.

Rayna then told me that the following Wednesday night I would be having my "sutures" removed, and gave me very specific instructions of precisely what I was to do in preparation for my eight hours of sleep while the entities removed their sutures. Of course I did exactly as I was instructed, but that modicum of doubt still swirled around in my mind about spirits removing invisible sutures. My friend told me that anything could happen and that when it took place for her the first time, the room actually shook like a minor earthquake, so I might want to remove anything valuable from high places in my bedroom in the event that I had the same experience.

Rayna sent me by FedEx (again from Brazil) water that had been blessed by John of God, which I was to place by my bedside. I was to wear white to bed, and pray and be pure love. As I dozed off I had a picture of everyone I could imagine in my mind, and I bathed them all in a cascade of pure love.

The next morning I looked at my watch, a watch that has a ten-day power supply source, a watch that has always kept perfect time to the second. It was 7:05 A.M. The phone next to my bed rang, and my dear friend Kerry asked me how the night went. I told her I was just waking up, and she said, "But it's 8:25 A.M. I'm at the airport!"

I assured her that her time was incorrect, and she was adamant that it was 8:25. It turns out that my precision-guaranteed watch had stopped for 80 minutes during the night! When I walked out to the kitchen, my children jokingly asked if I'd been doing drugs—my pupils were tiny, my left eye appeared to be scratched, my eyes were watering, and I looked to them as if something very strange had happened to me. *I felt like I was pure love.* Everything I looked at I saw with new eyes: the tree was love, my plants were love, the ocean was love, and every person I saw that day, I just wanted to tell them how much I loved them. I was a walking being of love, and it has not dissolved since then.

Two days later, that same precision watch once again inexplicably lost exactly 80 minutes. Then the next day, Rayna called and told me that the clock on her automobile was 80 minutes slower than it was supposed to be, and she sent me a photo verifying it. I have no idea what transpired in those 80 minutes. Rayna hypothesized that the electromagnetic field of the healing energies from the entities doing the surgical procedures through John of God is so much more powerful than the field of the watch that I was wearing, that while they were healing and removing the sutures it caused the watch to stop. I admit I can't give an intelligent answer, other than I was being given absolute proof in a physical way that what was taking place was not only real, but that I would be able to tell others of this phenomenon because I live such a visible life. At any rate, my body has still been detoxifying. I am feeling so much love for everyone, including a person who engaged in litigation against me, attempting to achieve financial gain—something that once made me angry—and now all I can do is bathe him in love as well. (And the litigation ended shortly thereafter as well.)

At this point I would like to go back to my discussion of the orb phenomenon that has recently infiltrated my life. The Heinemanns' book contains 65 color photos with orbs in them, taken at various functions all over the world. After my experience with John of God, I learned that some of those photos were sent to the authors showing orbs making themselves visible in photos taken in Abadiania. They are reproduced in the photo insert.

Note the huge orb above John of God (João de Deus) while he does a visible healing intervention, and a photo where the orbs cloud the image of the entire healing encounter. The presence of these orbs with John of God, as well as those that seem to be showing up at my speaking events, is a synchronicity that defies my reasoning powers. Yet it is there, and I am open to learning what it all means, or living with contentment in the mystery. What I can report with certainty is that profound changes have taken place in my body in both a physical sense, and even more emphatically, in a feeling sense.

When I received the diagnosis of leukemia, I had been told by several physicians that I wouldn't be able to continue practicing Bikram yoga four days a week. The heat, I was informed, would be way too strenuous and it would be ill-advised for me to continue this activity. Sure enough, I found myself feeling so weak in yoga class that I ultimately abandoned the practice.

Yet one early morning while meditating, just 20 days following my suture removal, I heard an inner voice saying, *Do not go for a walk today. You can now do yoga.* I listened, and went to my first

Bikram yoga class in 11 months. Although I was rusty, I completed the class, much to my renewed joy. I had always loved yoga, and I had missed it terribly. I am back to an early-morning class, four times a week, and my ability to hold the postures in the heat have surpassed what I was accomplishing prior to my leukemia diagnosis. I feel stronger, and those aches and pains that had returned when I abandoned yoga are completely gone.

A few days later, I celebrated my 71st birthday in a totally unique way. The overwhelming sense of love I felt after my experience with the healing entities was dominating my every waking moment. That day I went out on the streets of San Francisco and talked with an array of homeless people. I felt compelled to simply love and give; to that end, I had a wad of cash with me, and I passed out $50 bills to at least 30 different somewhat lost souls. When I returned to my hotel room, I sat on the bed and simply sobbed in gratitude. I have never had such a memorable birthday, a day in which I felt driven to reach out and give love, without any expectations in return.

I now feel absolutely imbued by love. And while my body seems to be detoxing, I've shifted my eating habits, and my body feels cleaner and healthier. I have not partaken of new blood tests and medical evaluations, because I trust in what I experienced to such a degree that I need no external validation to assure me that these mysterious mystical events took place. I was there for the surgery, and I was there for the suture removal. I need say nothing more.

I believe in miracles, and I also know that I am not this outer body. I have no fear of death because I am birthless, deathless, and changeless. This is my *I am* presence of being one with God. In addition to this feeling, it has become clear to me since my John of God experience that I am more and more in contact with what I can only label *angelic guidance*.

In my morning meditations, I receive what feels like instruction on how to conduct my day. Without exception, when I follow this guidance I find myself encountering amazing opportunities to reach out and serve, and my inner voice says, *Follow through and be of service.* One recent morning provides an example of what I'm experiencing daily.

By 6:30 A.M. I'd conversed with a man who was struggling in his marriage. I advised him to focus for the next 24 hours on unconditional love. It was an unexpected, unplanned encounter, and I gifted him two books and a copy of my movie, *The Shift.* He was elated and expressed that he felt a huge burden had been lifted from his body as a result of our conversation.

On my way back home, I encountered a homeless young man asleep on the beach, gifted him $100, and talked to him passionately about seeking help for his drug addiction. He smiled from ear to ear and said that I was the first person he met on Maui who wasn't full of judgment toward him.

When I got home, I discovered I'd taken the wrong key and was unable to enter my apartment. On the way to the desk to retrieve a correct key, I encountered a woman who had lost her son in an automobile accident some two years earlier. As we talked she told me how, just the day before, she had seen for the first time a video of his second-grade graduation, which was sent to her by a friend. Tears came to her eyes as she described having to testify in a few days at the sentencing of the impaired driver who caused her son's death. We walked together to get the new key, and I invited her into my home. I then gave her a copy of Anita Moorjani's description of her NDE in which she defines death as an awareness of coming into the light of pure love. I said to this woman that after reading Anita's account, she might have some of her anguish removed.

I feel these three experiences of synchronicity were the outcome of my hearing and responding to angelic guidance during meditation, directing me to walk in a certain direction at a certain time. Three people's lives were touched because I was not only told where and when to walk, but also because I felt compelled by inner persuasive forces to reach out and be of service. These kinds of synchronicities as a result of inner callings happen every day since my experience of healing with the entities working through John of God. I observe, I listen, and I act—and I feel as if I'm a *being of love* more than just a *loving being.*

What I have noticed is that I feel as though I learned the lesson of assuming the feeling of the wish fulfilled. I am not simply a loving person, *I am love.* I was transformed in the encounters with John of God, and I rejoice in giving love to everyone and everything I encounter.

This word, *feeling,* is so crucial for you to embrace. In *The "I AM" Discourses,* this point is vividly made: "I say to you, beloved Minute Men and friends of America, when you understand there is not one thing in the whole universe that can touch you, limit you, or harm you but that which acts through your own *feeling world,* then will you come into the fullness of life. You cannot do it until you do realize that."[58] My healing experiences with John of God, I believe, made me realize that.

The Third Personal Experience

My third event involves the enigmatic subject of past lives—or parallel lives, since time doesn't really exist in an infinite universe. My good friend and colleague Brian Weiss has written, researched, and lectured extensively on this topic, and I have been pleased to share the stage with him in venues all over the world. His groundbreaking book *Many Lives, Many Masters* was my first real introduction to past-life regression, and while I have seldom had any firsthand experience in this area, I've always found reincarnation and past lives a fascinating area of inquiry.

Several months ago I received an invitation to participate in a past-life hypnotic regression from a woman who had worked with Dr. Weiss. Her letter indicated that she intuitively felt I would benefit from a session conducted by her, and she would be willing to come to Maui and do the hypnotic life regression if I were willing.

Her name is Dobromira Kelley, and like Rayna and my initiatic teacher whom I refer to throughout this book, Omraam Mikhaël Aïvanhov, she was born in Bulgaria. She goes by the name of Mira, and is a practicing attorney in New York City. Her letter was so detailed, well written, honest, and compassionate that I elected to contact her and see what she was proposing.

Mira told me that she felt compelled to offer this to me. She'd heard me lecture in NYC, read several of my books, and was aware of the health issues concerning my diagnosis of chronic lymphocytic leukemia. She wanted nothing—only to offer me this opportunity—and it was a heartfelt thing with her and a calling that she wouldn't ignore.

A few weeks later I received a package in the mail containing Anita Moorjani's description of her NDE experience. Mira's decision to send me this interview with Anita was synchronistic in so many ways. It moved me to the point that I had copies made and gave them to many people, including my 95-year-old mother who lives in an assisted-living center. My mother simply loved what Anita shared about her experience of being in a coma, being on "the other side," and her miraculous healing from a diagnosis of certain death on the horizon within the next 36 hours. It is the same NDE depiction that I gave to the mother whose eight-year-old son had been killed by an impaired driver.

Since that time I have come to know Anita, who is now cancer-free. Her story, *Dying to Be Me,* has been published by Hay House, and she's appeared on my radio show and appears on my latest PBS special, telling her story for the entire world to hear. And as I mentioned previously, I'm privileged to have written the Foreword for her book.

Anita told me that she feels the reason she had her NDE and returned from the very edge of death to have a miraculous recovery was to tell the world what she learned while in that state of God-realized awareness. We both feel that our meeting, and arranging to have her story published and appear with me on television, is part of God's plan for her and myself as well. Mira Kelley's decision to send Anita's NDE report to me was a vital link in this stupendous chain of events.

I told Mira by telephone that I would be here for several consecutive weeks the following month, but I couldn't commit to a firm appointment. She said fine, and I pretty much left it alone. Then one day she called and told me that she was on Maui and would be available any time in the next week. We set a time for Thursday at 10 A.M.—exactly one week prior to my surgery from John of God, which hadn't even been scheduled yet. At that time, Rayna was in Brazil and didn't have a commitment from John of God to perform the long-distance surgery.

At precisely 10 A.M. on Thursday, Mira knocked at my door, and within one hour I was entering into one of the most riveting three hours of hypnotic time traveling imaginable. Mira recorded the entire session, and also transcribed every word in a script format. I reproduce a portion of that experience for you to read and engage in opening your mind to infinite possibilities:

Wayne: Desert. I see mountains of sand . . . people dressed in desert garb, Arab garb of some kind.

Mira: Very good. Are you outside or looking from inside out?

Wayne: Outside. There are a lot of people walking around. Lots of heavy clothes on.

Mira: Are you in a place in a town where people live?

Wayne: No. It's . . . I guess like a village of some kind, just a bunch of tents. People walking around. Men with beards, women with their faces covered.

Mira: Yeah. Look down at your feet and tell me what your feet are dressed in or if they have anything.

Wayne: My feet are barefeet.

Mira: Barefeet. . . . How about your legs? Do you have clothes on your legs?

Wayne: I just have on like a shirt, a T-shirt of some kind. I actually don't have very much on at all.

Mira: How does the clothing feel against your skin? Does it feel like refined cloth or does it feel rougher?

Wayne: I am not sure I have anything on, to tell you the truth.

Mira: What does your energy feel like?

Wayne: Like a diaper on. But I'm not a baby.

Mira: Does your energy feel like male energy?

Wayne: Yeah.

Mira: Do you feel young or old?

Wayne: I feel 11, 12.

Mira: Stretch your hand in front of you and see if you have any jewelry or anything on your hands.

Wayne: No . . . I see a green ruby. I guess I maybe do have. It's a green ruby . . . hmm. That's weird. It's green.

Mira: Is there anything around your neck? I mean, decorations?

Wayne: No.

Mira: Right. How about your face and your head, how do they feel?

Wayne: It just feels young . . . like a little boy's face. Blond.

Mira: Do you have anything on your head?

Wayne: I just have a rag thing or something. Like a cloth of some kind. It's just, um . . .

Mira: Let's walk around these tents and see what else is going on around you.

Wayne: I just see a lot of people shuffling around. It feels like Afghanistan. It seems someplace like that. Tribal kinds of people with beards, but I'm just very young. And I don't look like they do.

Mira: Do they look different than you?

Wayne: They look old with beards. Women's faces are covered.

Mira: Let's go up to your tent and see where you sleep at night.

Wayne: I don't . . . I don't think I belong here. I think I'm just kind of wandering. I don't feel like I have a home here. I feel like they don't even notice me, though. Even like I'm invisible to them.

Mira: Let's go a little back in time before this scene and see where you come from, how did you get there.

Wayne: I think I just wandered. I think I was just wandering and living in the woods or something. Nobody seems to notice me.

Mira: Let's go a little forward then and see what happens next.

Wayne: I'm looking for food. I'm very thin. And I have . . . you can see my ribs.

Mira: How do you usually find food?

Wayne: Just eating things like apples and fruits . . . whatever is growing in the woods.

Mira: Do you have family or are you by yourself?

Wayne: I'm by myself. Seems like my family has been ambushed or something.

Mira: You can see that. Just go back and let the knowledge emerge.

Wayne: I think . . . I don't think I've had family for a long time. I think my family was killed by invaders of some kind. I ran away and escaped.

Mira: Let's go a little forward to another moment in the lifetime and see what happens.

Wayne: I'm . . . I can't get anyone to notice me. I'm looking for clothes, for something to keep me warm. So I steal them and no one notices.

Mira: Do you still have the ruby on your finger?

Wayne: It's green.

Mira: How did you get it?

Wayne: I found it.

Mira: You found it? That's a good treasure to find. What do you do with it?

Wayne: It's meaningless. It doesn't mean anything to me. I feel like I'm lost and I can't get anyone to realize what has happened. I ran away for a long time. I have sores on me and cuts.

Mira: Tell me about these sores and these cuts. How did they come to be?

Wayne: I think from scratches from the trees, thorns, and bushes. Wandering through that kind of brush. I haven't eaten in a while.

Mira: What do you do next?

Wayne: I'm going up to people and asking. I'm just invisible to them. They don't know I'm there. I could take anything I wanted. I'm like a ghost. Pale. Just wearing a little loincloth. I'm not afraid at all. Just can't figure out why nobody is paying attention.

Mira: Let's go a little forward and see what happens next.

Wayne: I just gather up fruits and figs and dried fruit, oranges, apricots. And I have no pockets to stuff them in, so I just take this tray of treasures and go back. That doesn't make any sense. I just go back into the brush.

Mira: And that's where you eat them?

Wayne: Yeah, but I'm . . . I think I had a sister, and I think she's still alive. I want to take this stuff back to her and find her.

Mira: Is she there when you go back? Or are you looking for her now?

Wayne: Yeah, I'm wandering. Looking back . . . there's a fireplace, and the fire is out. There are bodies around. People have been killed. My father's been killed. He's old. There's women weeping.

Mira: Has your mom been killed as well?

Wayne: I don't have a mom.

Mira: How about any other family? Your sister?

Wayne: She's hiding by an older woman. I guess it's her grandmother. I think her mother has been gone. She's been taken away. She's little. She's younger than me. She's got blonde hair.

Mira: How do you feel seeing all this?

Wayne: Sick. Angry. Sad. And I bring her food— the apricots, the dried apricot, oranges, and she's only three, four.

Mira: What do you call her?

Wayne: Samantha. Sam. Sammy.

Mira: And how does she call you when she wants to speak with you?

Wayne: She just smiles. She doesn't talk.

Mira: Let's go a little forward and see what happens to her and to you.

Wayne: She's too afraid to move, and I feel we have to get out of there. I try to persuade her that we have to leave, but she doesn't want to leave. The old people are still unharmed, grieving. I can see dead bodies around me in this enclave that is there.

Mira: Has it been more than your father who has been killed?

Wayne: That's my father. He's lying there helpless. He's dead. Blood coming out of his mouth. He makes no sound. It's so weird. His grandmother is dressed like an Arab woman. My father had a pair of brown pants on, a belt, no shoes, and the pants only come to his calves. They're tight. He had no shirt on. And he's been ambushed. And the grandmother is just dressed in all black clothes.

Mira: What are the old people saying to each other? What do they think has happened?

Wayne: The women are just crying. They have obviously been attacked, and I'm just bewildered by how I am going to take care of this mess.

Mira: What do you do next?

Wayne: I try to find something to dig with to bury my father because there are flies flying around his body now.

Mira: Do you find anything?

Wayne: Just some pieces of wood. And I try to find a place to put him in.

Mira: Is anybody helping you?

Wayne: No, there's nobody to help me. I'm alone here except for my little sister with these pigtails.

Mira: And now let's go forward in time to another important day and see what happens in this lifetime.

Wayne: I actually just leave, I just leave and take care of that.

Mira: Do you leave your sister behind?

Wayne: Yeah, I think I do. I can't believe it, but I do.

Mira: And where do you go?

Wayne: I go to the sea. I go to a place where there's a lot of boats. It's before modern boats. It's like tall masted boats.

Mira: What do you do?

Wayne: I'm older now. I get passage to someplace, but

I don't know where. And I agree to work. I don't know where I'm going. I don't know where the ship is going. I don't know these people. I don't speak their language.

Mira: What kind of work do you do on the ship?

Wayne: I'm working in the galley. I think it's going to Greece.

Mira: See the ship arriving and you getting off, and see where you are.

Wayne: I'm much older. I'm 22. Strong. No shirt. Like a knapsack with all my possessions, which is almost nothing, and boots . . . same kind of pants my father had on.

Mira: Where do you go next? What do you do next?

Wayne: I'm just looking for a place to stay. And these people befriend me who live in a hut. Greek.

Mira: What does the hut look like?

Wayne: It looks like an igloo without ice, just sort of round. Trying to figure out when this is.

Mira: Who lives in the hut?

Wayne: A husband and a wife and . . . that's it. A man and a wife. Older people. And they love me very much. They work the land. Agricultural. Olives. Olive trees. Grapes. Very poor. Lot of dust. I stay there. I don't like working the land. I go into the village, and I don't want to work the land. I don't want to do that.

I meet a woman who works at . . . serving wine, I think it's wine. And I don't drink it. These casks, these containers of liquid . . . she pours it into the cups. I'm attracted to her. She has the face of . . . it's clearly her. And we fall in love. This little Greek . . . she's got long black hair, very narrow face. And a little mouth. And big eyes.

And she's young: 16, 17, 18. She just flirts and wants to know why I'm dressed the way I am, why I look the way I do and how I look so different from her. Because I'm fair, and she's not. She holds my hand. And I fall in love with her. Almost instantly. And I take a job on a ship, and leave. We're married.

And the ship is going all the way to the New World. It's explorers. There's talk of islands and people who live on them all across the sea. And that excites me. And I go, and I leave her. She's pregnant. But I leave anyway. That just sounds so enticing to find something that no one's ever seen before. It's like a great adventure. And I'm gone for a long time. Like years. We go to . . . we discover natives and new things, new people. A lot of people dying at sea, bodies are being thrown out at sea. A lot of scurvy, a lot sickness, a lot of vomiting, a lot of people dying. And we find a place. Española? I don't know what that means. Dark people.

Mira: Do you find that in the middle of the ocean?

Wayne: Yeah. After months, six, seven, eight months of sea. Just eating few berries and things that are left. We finally hit land. I have a beard. But I'm strong. A lot of people dying. But I'm not dying. I keep surviving.

Mira: What does this place look like?

Wayne: It looks like an island. Native people. Lots of trees, coconut trees. Lush. Lots of fresh fruit. Natives that are friendly, but we're not. This captain and these people running this thing are just really vicious and cruel to these people. It's hard for me to imagine that they would do such a thing. I try to persuade them not to. They kill people with machetes and knives and things. They're just vicious to these people for no reason. Just because they're different. Can't comprehend that. And they load up the ship, but I don't participate in any of the killing and the violence. These people look African, so they are native. I can't figure out why we are so cruel to them.

Mira: What do you do next? Do you continue exploring or do you go back?

Wayne: No. We load up. Someone makes notes on where this is. And I can't figure this out because I don't know anything about how to figure all that stuff out. I can't figure out how they'd find a place in the middle of the ocean. But a lot of fishing with lines. Then we go back. And it takes six, seven months to get back again. I want to see my wife, but when I get back, I can't find her.

Mira: What happened to her?

Wayne: She died.

Mira: What did she die of?

Wayne: Some kind of sickness in her chest. She couldn't breathe.

Mira: Did she die before she had the child?

Wayne: There's supposedly a little boy, but no one knows what happened to him. Two years old, but no one knows anything. They're all telling me that she waited and waited and waited for me, but I was just gone for so long. I'm much older now. Got gray. I was gone for a long time. Ten years.

Mira: How do you feel knowing that you cannot find her and that she has died?

Wayne: Very sad. Very guilty.

Mira: Let move forward and see what happens next.

Wayne: I just get very sad and depressed. Trying to figure why there's so much violence around me, so much killing. Why can't people just . . . it's just a mystery that everybody wants to hurt everybody. I think I write about it. I have to tell. It seems like such a futile thing. Everybody is just so violent, everybody hates everybody. There's hardly any love anywhere. Everybody is just into surviving, trying to take something from somebody else. Trying to talk to people, about just . . . caring about each other. And I want to write about it.

Mira: How do you do that? How do you talk to people? Do you talk to them one-on-one, or do you stand somewhere?

Wayne: No. I just write down what seems to make sense and figure that someway, somehow people are going to get the message. It just seems that anytime anybody settles down and everything gets sorted out, somebody just comes in and starts killing people, chopping heads off. I'm always perplexed by that. I just can't figure out what in the world . . . why would people do this to each other? I'm just mystified, always mystified, at the cruelty that people seem to show to everybody, even the people who are in their family, living close in the same villages, they're still fighting with each other.

It just seems like I'm outside of all of that. I don't have any fights. I don't have any case against anybody. I just want to be left alone, let people be left alone, let them live the way they will, not trying to impose something on them. No one seems to get that. It just seems like that's a foreign idea to everybody. I'm really thought of as a crazy old man because I talk about. . . .

I'm writing and there's a light, big light, white light . . . it's like I'm in a cave, and that's the only place I can get any peace. There's a light that comes into the cave right through the roof, through the ceiling. I just sit there, and . . . what do I write on? I write on tablets of some kind. They look like stone. And these truths are just coming right through the ceiling into this light, and they just seem so obvious to me. I can't figure out why they're coming to me. It's like I have this special pipeline to whatever this light is. This light is really bright. It is really bright right now. I feel like I'm Socrates. It doesn't seem like the right time. I'm this wise old man. I've got a white beard to here. And I've got like a whole white robe. It's like something the Pope would wear almost. These things that are coming are so . . .

Mira: How does it feel when they come? Does it feel like ideas?

Wayne: No, they come in pictures. Love is the thing. It's just love. And the word *love* and the feeling of love. Then the hypocrisy of it all. Nobody, like these are the things that I am the only one who knows. Nobody else knows this.

Mira: How do you share it with people? Do you travel around?

Wayne: No, I'm just sitting in a cave, and this information is coming to me, and it just makes me light. It's like a knowing. I know I'm going to die soon. And I feel compelled to leave this information in some way, and I'm perplexed by how to do that, how to get these truths just coming through this cave.

I'm telling you—I'm in a cave. There's a roof above me, but the light just comes right through this cave. It's all dark in there, but there's a light that looks like this, like a spotlight. It goes like this, starts narrow and goes wider and wider and wider. Out of this light comes these truths. All these truths are just about love. They're just about love. That's the only word I can see: L-O-V-E. Get this message out there. Get this message out there. You just have to love each other. If you could just get that, all this pain and this killing, all this violence, this hatred, it's so simple, it just seems so simple to me. I just have this awakening. It's like . . . wow.

All I have to do is just convince people to do this, but then I look inside myself and know that no one is going to believe it. It's all just going to be bullshit to everybody. No one is going to accept this. But yet you know it's this profound truth. You just have to love each other. Just love each other, and you can have your wife back, you can have your sister back.

And now she's back. She's back. I can see her whole life unfolding right before me. And my wife is back. And I can see her smiling and how much she loved me. She wished I wouldn't have left. My sister wished I wouldn't have left. My father . . . and I'm just so heartbroken because I know that nobody is going to get this. Nobody gets this.

And I can't persuade people. They're just so hell-bent on survival and fearing that somebody else is going to come and take what's theirs because that's what everybody does. They create armies and build up all this hatred over all of this stuff . . . over little, meager pieces of fruit, little nothing, over the few things that they have, the few crops that they have. I just can't get it. Why don't you just share those things with each other instead of hoarding? You'll multiply them. That's one of the truths that come right through the light. If you share . . .

Mira: If you share, there'll be more?

Wayne: Nobody gets it. If you share it, you multiply it. If you hoard it, you lose it. It just seems like such a simple thing. Yet it's just so . . . nobody can, nobody can . . . it goes against everything. Everybody laughs. What an absurd idea that is. If you share it, you lose it. No. If you share it, you'll have more. Nobody seems to get it. Everyone just wants to take theirs and get it before somebody else does.

And we bury people, and we kill people. And there is a head over here, a leg over there. It's like . . . I've seen so much of that. It's just so clear, this truth is just so clear. This truth is just so clear, so clear. You just have to love each other. Love yourself. Love each other. You're going to be crucified for that, though. You're going to be laughed at. You are going to be an outcast.

Now I look back and even as a little boy, I knew it. I don't want to hurt anybody. I just wanted to feed people. I just wanted to talk sensibly to these crazy people who have swords and they want to do so much damage. I'm just a little boy saying . . . they wanted to kill me and they just stopped and let me run away. They killed my father instead. They took my mother someplace. God knows what happened to her.

Mira: When you're in the cave and you receive these truths, see yourself being there, and see how you write them. See your hands and what's in front of you.

Wayne: The truth of it is, I see them and want to record it. But I feel like it's a waste of time to write it down.

Mira: Right. Because people won't believe you?

Wayne: Nobody does. They only know taking care of themselves. They only know themselves. There's so little sharing. And so it's . . . my son has come there. I'm not gonna write this down. I don't write it down. I just tell him.

Mira: How did you find him?

Wayne: He's 30 years old . . . more . . . 40 years old . . . 50 years old . . . I'm very old.

Mira: So you tell him these truths?

Wayne: I tell him to remember these things. That these are great truths. That when you share, you multiply.

191

When you hoard, you lose. When you do less to other people, you get more. That being humble and gentle, and soft, you get so much more. I'm telling you. You get so close to God. That light is God coming through there. That light is God. It is just so bright.

I can see it. Here it comes again. It starts up here, and it goes like this. You just swim in it. You just bathe in this light. It's all so easy. Just tell them that this is easy. It's not hard. It's natural. It's normal. It's what you came from. It's what you are. Find out what you are, and be that. Don't find out what you aren't and try to be that. It's just another truth. One of those simple, simple truths. Be who you are instead of who you're not.

And you can't be anything other than what you are anyway. It is an illusion. If you try to be something that you are not, you can't be anything you're not. You're not hate, you're not killing. That's not who you are. Be who you are. All of that other stuff is not who you are . . . just be who you are.

My son looks perplexed. He thinks I'm a crazy old man. I am a crazy old man. Everyone around me . . . the only one who understood this was, oh my goodness, that beautiful woman. I only knew her for such a short time. And then I left her. She knew this. She waited. She didn't die of something in her chest. She was killed.

My son just told me that. She was killed, too, while I was gone. Everything you love, you lose when you lose the love. Everything you love you lose when you lose the love. So simple. She was murdered, raped. My son wants to know how I feel about the rapist.

"How do you feel, Dad, about the people who killed the woman you love?"

And the light is there. And you can go into it or you can go around it. When you go into it, there's only love, and if I try to go around, it's dark. And it makes me want to kill those motherfuckers.

When I go into the light, I love the rapists. When you lose the love, that's it. When you lose the love, you lose who you are because who you are is love. And all the rest of the time you wander around in the darkness just trying to avoid the light, which just calls you, pulls you toward it. It wants to be in it so much. It's too bright. It blinds you with its brightness.

You can really love the people who kill the woman you love. I guess . . . I guess I can because that's who I am. When you love, there's just no room for anything else. If you love, there's just no such thing as nonlove. It's all you have to give away. It's when you leave the spotlight, when you leave the light that's coming into this cave . . . see it come in like this, and then there's all these dark places around it.

And you want me to go into the dark places. But I can't. Because I am the same as that light. That's who I am. And it saddens me, but it seems to me that's what I'm here for.

He tells me that she loved me so much. She waited and waited and waited, and I let her down. Because I had to seek out my adventure. I had to find the new places. And all the while I didn't leave to go anywhere.

He says he can't do it. And I say to him, "You're just not ready, but it is who you are, too."

And I got up, and walked into that light. I can see it now. And I left him, too . . . bewildered. And I went into that light, and I let myself float into it. I looked down at him, "My son, just move over a few inches into the light. It's just a few inches away. Just slide over, and you'll be in the light. Here is the light and you are here. Just move over here. You just have to move this far."

You know what he said? "Fuck you. You crazy old man. I'm going to get those guys."

That's all. I'm sick. I feel like I'm going to throw up.

Mira: Just take a deep breath.

Wayne: I need water.

Mira: I'll get you some.

Wayne: Oh my God. Oh my goodness.

Mira: Just lay down again. Very good. Just close your eyes. Let this light now absorb all the emotions, all the energy, let it all resolve within your body. Let it all turn into love. Let it all get healed. Very good. Just be in that cave again with that beautiful light above you. Just stay in the light. Let it wash over you. Now tell me, after your son leaves, what happens next?

Wayne: Well . . . I don't exist anymore, I'm just formless.

Mira: You can see everything . . . everything that happened. What do you think is the purpose you had in the lifetime to learn and to share?

Wayne: It wasn't about learning and sharing. It was about being. I had to learn to be it instead of trying to become it. I had to learn to be it. And it took me to the end of that life to get that. Because now I am God, I'm with God. It all just seems so trivial.

While I had almost no memory of precisely what I said during this session, the visual images are still crystal clear. Was it a reflection of a past life, a parallel life? I can only speculate on that, but I am intrigued by what I said and what transpired while I was in that semihypnotic state with Mira. As Anita Moorjani said to me in a recent letter, "When I am willing to step into the realm of uncertainty and ambiguity, I open myself up to infinite possibilities." I leave you to ponder this mystery.

Question #7: Am I Willing to Meditate to the I Am That I Am Frequencies?

James Twyman, the author of *The Moses Code,* asked sound-healing expert Jonathan Goldman to research and create tuning forks that encode the holy name of God—and then reproduce these frequencies in a meditation program. The basis of these recordings is tuning forks that Jonathan designed. They correspond to the gematria of the holy name *I am that I am* given to Moses at the burning bush, as detailed in the book of Exodus in the Old Testament.

At the end of *The Moses Code,* Jonathan explains how these frequencies were created to match the ancient Kabbalah tradition, wherein specific numbers are assigned to whole words and phrases. He concludes his remarks on his research in creating these meditation frequencies by writing: "The I AM THAT I AM tuning forks and the associated field created by them is a provocative and exciting sound experience, and the potential is promising."

Meditation is a vital practice to access conscious contact with your highest self. I have meditated for many years and wrote a book *(Getting in the Gap)* on the many benefits of meditation. When I use the Moses Code frequency meditation, I feel a deep sense of peace that echoes the messages I've written about in this book. I use the inner mantra *I am,* seeing myself as already having arrived at what I've placed in my mind. Then I repeat silently *I am,* the name of God given to Moses, honoring the cooperation of my highest self, and acknowledging my Divinely aligned desires. With these spiritually uplifting sounds wafting through the room or my earphones, I breathe in a sense of tranquility and conscious contact with God.

These frequencies have been a regular part of my meditation and manifesting spiritual activities for the past year or so. In fact, I meditate every day for 40 minutes using these exact frequencies to accompany me as I make conscious contact with God in my sacred meditation practice. I encouraged several of my children to join me in a meditation session listening to these sacred sounds while using the mantra *I am that I am*. After only one session, my adult children were hooked, and each day they would ask me to put on the "I am wishes fulfilled sounds," so that we could all meditate together.

I have reproduced the sacred sounds in a separate CD titled *I AM Wishes Fulfilled Meditation*. The CD contains three tracks. The first is an explanation of how to use this meditation and the results that have accrued to me. I practice daily with either headphones or not, in a room aglow with white candles. To me the sounds are sacred, and I am indebted to James Twyman and Jonathan Goldman for doing the extensive research to re-create these sounds that match up with the special numbers associated with the phrase *EHYEH ASHER EHYEH*. These were the words that God spoke to Moses when he asked for God's name as reported in the book of Exodus. These words in Hebrew are most often translated as "I am that I am."

Listening to the sacred sounds while meditating brings me, and some of my children as well, a sense of tranquility and a feeling of being at total oneness with the Divine. I simply love having these sounds with me in this holy practice of meditation as a tool in the whole process of living a wishes fulfilled life.

The second track is a 20-minute reproduction of the Moses Code Frequency Meditation, for a deep meditation, and the third track is a 20-minute meditation version with guitar accompaniment for a more active experience. I do tracks two and three consecutively every day, using the *I am that I am* mantra as explained in track one. It is indeed a very powerful tool for manifesting into your life all of your God-realized desires.

Summary

The Essence of Putting These Profound Teachings to Work in Your Life

1. Be willing to change your concept of yourself, which means changing what you have believed to be true.

2. Recognize yourself as always connected to your Source of being.

3. Become willing to say "I am God" from an egoless perspective.

4. Treasure your greatest gift—your imagination.

5. Live as if what you desire is already here.

6. Assume the feeling of your wish fulfilled.

7. Never let your attention be directed by anything or anyone other than your own highest self.

8. Use the last moments of your day before sleeping to reinforce in your mind your desires as fulfilled.

9. Have a mind that is open to all possibilities.

10. Remember always:

> *You were born with potential.*
> *You were born with goodness and trust.*
> *You were born with ideals and dreams.*
> *You were born with greatness.*
> *You were born with wings.*
> *You are not meant for crawling, so don't.*
> *You have wings.*
> *Learn to use them and fly.*
>
> — RUMI

This concludes my labor of love in bringing all of this material into print. I have been profoundly touched by the many spiritual teachers whom I have quoted throughout this book.

ENDNOTES

Special thanks goes to the Saint Germain Foundation, for permission to quote from *The "I AM" Discourses,* by Ascended Master Saint Germain, Volumes 3 and 11. (©Saint Germain Foundation, Schaumburg, IL—Used by Permission.) Please visit: **www.Saint GermainPress.com**.

Special thanks also goes to DeVorss Publications, for permission to quote from *The Power of Awareness* and *Feeling Is the Secret,* by Neville. (©DeVorss Publications, Camarillo, CA—Used by Permission.) Please visit: **www.DeVorss.com**.

Quotes from all of these wonderful books are noted below.

Chapter 1

1. Neville, *The Power of Awareness*, pg. 7. Camarillo, CA: DeVorss Publications, 2005.

2. Neville, *The Power of Awareness*, pg. 12.

3. Neville, *The Power of Awareness*, pg. 9.

Chapter 3

4. Neville, *The Power of Awareness*, pg. 121.

5. Neville, *The Power of Awareness*, pg. 122.

6. Ascended Master Saint Germain, *The "I AM" Discourses*, Volume 3, Foreword. Schaumburg, IL: Saint Germain Press.

7. Ascended Master Saint Germain, *The "I AM" Discourses*, Volume 3, Discourse 01.

8. Neville, *The Power of Awareness*, pg. 121.

9. Neville, *The Power of Awareness*, pg. 3.

10. Ascended Master Saint Germain, *The "I AM" Discourses*, Volume 3, Discourse 02.

Chapter 4

11. Ascended Master Saint Germain, *The "I AM" Discourses*, Volume 3, Discourse 16.

12. Neville, *The Power of Awareness*, pg. 45–46.

Chapter 5

13. Neville, *The Power of Awareness*, pg. 63–64.

14. Neville, *The Power of Awareness*, pg. 10.

15. Neville, *The Power of Awareness*, pg. 11.

16. Neville, *The Power of Awareness*, pg. 69.

17. Ascended Master Saint Germain, *The "I AM" Discourses*, Volume 3, Discourse 21.

Chapter 6

18. Neville, *The Feeling Is the Secret* in *The Neville Reader*. Camarillo, CA: DeVorss Publications, 2005.

19. Ibid.

20. Ibid.

21. Ibid.

22. Ibid.

23. Ibid.

24. Ibid.

25. Ibid.

26. Neville, *The Power of Awareness*, pg. 46.

27. Neville, *The Power of Awareness*, pg. 82–83.

28. Neville, *The Feeling Is the Secret*.

Chapter 7

29. Neville, *The Power of Awareness*, pg. 49.

30. Ibid.

31. Neville, *The Power of Awareness*, pg. 50.

32. Ibid.

33. Ascended Master Saint Germain, *The "I AM" Discourses*, Volume 3, Discourse 11.

34. Neville, *The Power of Awareness*, pg. 80.

35. Ascended Master Saint Germain, *The "I AM" Discourses*, Volume 3, Discourse 06.

36. Neville, *The Power of Awareness*, pg. 86.

37. Ascended Master Saint Germain, *The "I AM" Discourses*, Volume 3, Discourse 16.

38. Neville, *The Power of Awareness*, pg. 24.

Chapter 8

39. Neville, *The Feeling Is the Secret*.

40. Ibid.

41. Ibid.

42. Ascended Master Saint Germain, *The "I AM" Discourses*, Volume 3, Discourse 04.

43. Neville, *The Feeling Is the Secret*.

44. Ibid.

45. Ascended Master Saint Germain, *The "I AM" Discourses*, Volume 3, Discourse 16.

Chapter 9

46. Neville, *The Power of Awareness*, pg. 111–112.

47. Neville, *The Power of Awareness*, pg. 112.

48. Ascended Master Saint Germain, *The "I AM" Discourses*, Volume 3, Discourse 16.

49. Ibid.

50. Ascended Master Saint Germain, *The "I AM" Discourses*, Volume 3, Discourse 26.

51. Ibid.

52. Ibid.

53. Neville, *The Feeling Is the Secret.*

54. Ascended Master Saint Germain, *The "I AM" Discourses*, Volume 3, Discourse 27.

55. Neville, *The Feeling Is the Secret.*

56. Ascended Master Saint Germain, *The "I AM" Discourses*, Volume 3, Discourse 07.

57. Ascended Master Saint Germain, *The "I AM" Discourses*, Volume 3, Discourse 31.

58. Ascended Master Saint Germain, *The "I AM" Discourses*, Volume 11. Schaumburg, IL: Saint Germain Press.

ABOUT THE AUTHOR

Affectionately called the 'father of motivation' by his fans, **Dr Wayne W. Dyer** was an internationally renowned author, speaker and pioneer in the field of self-development. Over the four decades of his career he wrote more than 40 books, including *Manifest Your Destiny, Wisdom of the Ages, There's a Spiritual Solution to Every Problem* and the *New York Times* bestsellers *10 Secrets for Success and Inner Peace, The Power of Intention, Inspiration, Change Your Thoughts – Change Your Life, Excuses Begone!, Wishes Fulfilled* and *I Can See Clearly Now.* He also created numerous audio programmes and videos, and appeared on thousands of radio and television shows, including *The Today Show, The Tonight Show* and *Oprah.*

Wayne held a doctorate in educational counselling from Wayne State University, was an associate professor at St. John's University in New York and honoured a lifetime commitment to education and finding the Higher Self. In 2015 he left his body, returning to Infinite Source to embark on his next adventure.

www.drwaynedyer.com

NOTES

NOTES

NOTES

NOTES

NOTES

NOTES

NOTES

NOTES

HAY HOUSE TITLES OF RELATED INTEREST

YOU CAN HEAL YOUR LIFE, the movie,
starring Louise L. Hay & Friends
(available as a 1-DVD program and an expanded 2-DVD set)
Watch the trailer at: **www.LouiseHayMovie.com**

THE SHIFT, the movie,
starring Dr Wayne W. Dyer
(available as a 1-DVD program and an expanded 2-DVD set)
Watch the trailer at: **www.DyerMovie.com**

ALL IS WELL: Heal Your Body with Medicine, Affirmations, and Intuition,
by Louise L. Hay and Mona Lisa Schulz, MD, PhD
(available September 2012)

*THE BIOLOGY OF BELIEF: Unleashing the Power of Consciousness,
Matter & Miracles,* by Bruce Lipton, PhD

*DYING TO BE ME: My Journey from Cancer, to Near Death,
to True Healing,* by Anita Moorjani

*FROM PLAGUES TO MIRACLES: The Transformational
Journey of Exodus, from the Slavery of Ego to the Promised Land of Spirit,*
by Robert S. Rosenthal, MD

*MIRRORS OF TIME: Using Regression for Physical, Emotional, and
Spiritual Healing* (book-with-CD), by Brian L. Weiss, MD

*THE MOSES CODE: The Most Powerful Manifestation Tool
in the History of the World,* by James F. Twyman

ORBS: Their Mission and Messages of Hope,
by Klaus Heinemann, PhD, and Gundi Heinemann

*THE PERFECT GENE DIET: Use Your Body's Own Apo E Gene and an
Integrative Medicine Approach to Treat High Cholesterol, Weight Problems,
Heart Disease, Alzheimer's . . . and More,* by Pamela McDonald, NP

*THE POWER OF SELF-HEALING: Unlock Your Natural
Healing Potential in 21 Days,* by Dr Fabrizio Mancini

All of the above are available at your local bookstore,
or may be ordered by contacting Hay House (see overleaf).

HAY HOUSE

Look within

Join the conversation about latest products, events, exclusive offers and more.

 Hay House UK

 @HayHouseUK

 @hayhouseuk

 healyourlife.com

We'd love to hear from you!